THE VEGAN ARGUMENT

Why There Really Is An Answer For Everything

By Lee Fox-Smith

First Published 2017 by Attwood Press

An Atwood Press Publication
www.attwoodpress.com

ISBN 9781520697789

The Vegan Argument
Why There Really Is An Answer For Everything

By Lee Fox-Smith
Attwood Press
Copyright © Lee Fox-Smith

Follow Lee Fox-Smith and his written work at
www.epicanimalquest.com

This Book is dedicated to the Billions of animals that are abused and killed every year.

We see you, we hear you, we are trying, and we will never give up.

Until All Are Free…..

CONTENTS

INTRODUCTION   i

Chapter 1 - The Best Way To Help Animals   1
Chapter 2 - How To Use This Book   4
Chapter 3 - Expect Hostility   7
Chapter 4 - Leave The Trolls Under Their Bridge   9
Chapter 5 - Patience, Persistence, and Positivity   11
Chapter 6 - The Vegan Sales Process   13
Chapter 7 - Needs Means Desire   17

SECTION 1 - NATURE & BIOLOGY   20

      Chapter 8 - We Are carnivores   21
      Chapter 9 - We Have Canine Teeth To Eat Meat   24
      Chapter 10 - We Have Evolved To Eat Meat   27
      Chapter 11 - It's Tradition   31
      Chapter 12 - Large Brains Because of Eating Meat   33
      Chapter 13 - Top Of The Food Chain   35
      Chapter 14 - We Have Always Eaten Animals   37
      Chapter 15 - Eating Animals Is Instinctual   39
      Chapter 16 - Animals Eat Animals   42
      Chapter 17 - Natural Circle of Life   45
      Chapter 18 - Lions Eat Meat   47

SECTION 2 - TASTE   50

      Chapter 19 - Why Do Animals Taste So Good?   51
      Chapter 20 - I Like Meat   54
      Chapter 21 - I Don't Like Vegetables   57

SECTION 3 - NUTRITION & HEALTH — 60

Chapter 22 - Vegans Are Unhealthy — 61
Chapter 23 - Vegans Get Ill All The Time — 64
Chapter 24 - Where Do You Get Calcium? — 67
Chapter 25 - Where Do You Get Protein? — 69
Chapter 26 - You Can't get B12 In A Vegan Diet — 75
Chapter 27 - What About Vitamin D? — 81
Chapter 28 - What About Iron? — 83
Chapter 29 - Can't Digest Cellulose — 85

SECTION 4 - ENVIRONMENT — 87

Chapter 30 - Vegans Kill More Animals — 88
Chapter 31 - We Need Manure To Grow Food Crops — 91
Chapter 32 - Countryside Without Animals? — 93
Chapter 33 - Farming Doesn't Impact Environment — 96
Chapter 34 - We Would Have To Grow More Crops — 98
Chapter 35 - Extreme Environments Eat Meat — 101
Chapter 36 - Bacon VS Lettuce — 103
Chapter 37 - Vegans Kill Plants — 105
Chapter 38 - Vegans Eat Animals Food — 108
Chapter 39 - Care About Animals Not Humans — 110
Chapter 40 - What About Wars and Famine? — 113
Chapter 41 - The Economy Would Crash — 115
Chapter 42 - Vegans Are Destroying The Rainforests — 117

SECTION 5 - FARMING — 120

Chapter 43 - Animals Are Not Hurt In Farms — 121
Chapter 44 - Free Range Is Good For The Animals — 124
Chapter 45 - Organic Is Good — 127

Chapter 46 - Killed Humanely   129

Chapter 47 - Mistreated Animals Would not Produce   131

Chapter 48 - Grateful For The Animals Sacrifice   134

Chapter 49 - Animals Don't Know What's Happening   136

Chapter 50 - Farmers out of work   139

Chapter 51 - What If We Stop Eating Them?   143

Chapter 52 - Farmers Don't Hurt Their Animals   146

Chapter 53 - Animals Are Better Off In A Farm   148

Chapter 54 - Humanely Raised Is Good   150

Chapter 55 - It's Had A Good Life   154

SECTION 6 - VEGAN MYTHS   157

Chapter 56 - Veganism is a Religion   158

Chapter 57 - Veganism Is A Cult   161

Chapter 58 - Veganism is A Belief   163

Chapter 59 - Vegans Try To Force Beliefs On People   169

Chapter 60 - Vegans Use Propaganda   171

Chapter 61 - Children Taken Away From Vegans   173

Chapter 62 - Vegans Wear Wool & Leather   176

Chapter 63 - Vegans Like To Be Difficult   179

Chapter 64 - Vegans Are Elitist   181

Chapter 65 - Vegans Are Judgemental   183

Chapter 66 - Vegans Are Extreme   185

Chapter 67 - Vegans Care What Other People Eat   188

Chapter 68 - Vegans Use Computers   190

Chapter 69 - You Can't Be 100% Vegan   193

Chapter 70 - Not Enough To Make A Difference   196

SECTION 7 - MORALITY & BEHAVIOUR   199

Chapter 71 - It is Legal   200

Chapter 72 - Vegans Mental Health Suffers   202

Chapter 73 - Food That Looks and Tastes Like Meat   205

Chapter 74 - It's A Personal Choice   207

Chapter 75 - Respect My Decision   209

Chapter 76 - Humans More Important Than Animals   212

Chapter 77 - What About Human Suffering?   214

Chapter 78 - That's What Animals Are For   217

Chapter 79 - But I'm Vegetarian   220

Chapter 80 - Pig Island   222

Chapter 81 - Morally obligated to promote veganism? 226

SECTION 8 - OTHER ARGUMENTS   231

Chapter 82 - Hunters Take The Place Of Predators   232

Chapter 83 - We Use Every Part Of The Animal   234

Chapter 84 - Eating Meat Advanced Civilisation   237

Chapter 85 - Agree To Disagree   239

Chapter 86 - Live and Let Live   241

Chapter 87 - It's Too Expensive To Go Vegan   243

Chapter 88 - Hitler Was A Vegetarian   246

Chapter 89 - Plants Hear Themselves Being Eaten   248

Chapter 90 - Tomatoes Scream When Cut   250

Chapter 91 - Soy, Labido, Sperm, and Penis Growth 252

Chapter 92 - No Puss In Milk   254

Chapter 93 - Fish Don't Feel Pain   256

Chapter 94 - Lobsters Don't Feel Pain   258

Chapter 95 - Eggs From Pets   262

Chapter 96 - Wool Must Be OK?   267

Chapter 97 - We Need Zoos   269

Chapter 98 - Horse Riding   271

Chapter 99 - Vegans Have Pets   273

A FINAL NOTE   275
ABOUT EPIC ANIMAL QUEST   276
FURTHER READING   280

INTRODUCTION

You have the power to change the world. I am not saying this lightly and it's not a cliche, you really can change the world. You have an idea that can be communicated in a way that resonates with millions of other compassionate people. Your idea is shared by others. When people come together with passion and determination, change can happen.

This book is primarily for Vegans. I have written this book to help Vegans answer the many questions that they are presented with on a daily basis. Some people just want to find out more about what being a Vegan really means. Others want to debate ideas. Some are meat eaters, farmers, vegetarians, even other vegans. My philosophy is that meat eaters, farmers, and vegetarians are not our enemies. Everyone who eats meat, eggs, or dairy, are just like we were, as most vegans were at one time, not vegan! I believe that being a vegan is foremost about helping the animals and the best way to do this is to speak for them as we would want to spoken for if we were in their position.

I decided to write this book just as if I was talking to a friend who had some questions about my choice to go vegan. It isn't snarky, or rude, or even disrespectful to people who choose to eat animals, but it is honest and to the point. I have tried my best to be rational, logical, and sensible throughout the book and included a bibliography for further reading and more information so you can explore the ideas further.

If you are not a Vegan, then I really think this book will be helpful to you too. The whole point of this book is to answer questions about Veganism. So if you eat meat or are a vegetarian and are interested in becoming a vegan, I hope this book will answer many of your questions. The fact that you have taken the time to read the introduction and consider buying this book, shows that you are already interested in Veganism and ready to help animals. There are many myths surrounding the Vegan lifestyle and diet, all of which are easily answered and shown to be false.

I am passionate about helping the animals and my family and I have dedicated our lives to the vegan movement. We run a social enterprise called Epic Animal Quest, where we travel around the world helping animal shelters and sanctuaries and we are doing our best to lead by example to show kindness, care, compassion, and peace to all creatures. You can find out more information about this at www.epicanimalquest.com

I hope this book will inspire you to talk confidently and proudly about being a vegan and give you the information you need to sow many seeds of compassion in many minds. You should never feel like you can't talk about being a vegan. You are on the side of justice, truth, and compassion, and you are the voice of the voiceless. Without you, the animals are helpless, but you can make a difference. When individuals like us join together with a common goal, spurred on without incentive, profit, or gain, only focusing on helping the helpless, then together, we really can change the world for the animals.

Thank you so much for everything you are doing to help the animals and thank you for choosing my book to be part of your vegan journey. Please enjoy reading and I would love it if you joined me on Twitter www.twitter.com/epicanimalquest Facebook https://www.facebook.com/epicanimalquest/ or got in touch by email lee@epicanimalquest.com

Thank you

Lee

CHAPTER 1

THE BEST WAY TO HELP ANIMALS

"It's not enough to be compassionate, you must act."

- Dalai Lama

What is the best way for us to help the animals? The first thing that comes to my mind is to simply stop eating them! This has a huge impact on the amount of animals killed every year and the more people that go vegan, the fewer animals are killed. Over 150 billion animals are killed every year just for us to eat them. If we can get the vegan population from 1% to 10%, imagine how fewer animals will have to die just to satisfy peoples habits, taste, convenience, and tradition?

It is something most people in the world can choose to do immediately. So what is holding them back? Unfortunately, eating meat comes with a long history of habit, tradition, convenience, and taste. Breaking habits is difficult, especially if the person has no desire to do so, but don't give up hope, information is power and armed with the right information it is possible to show people the importance of going vegan.

So if the answer is to stop eating animals, how can we encourage more people to do just that? Well, that's what this book is all about. It's about helping people to understand why vegans choose the vegan lifestyle and why it is better for the animals, the planet, and our health. It's about showing how eating, wearing, exploiting, and abusing animals is morally unjustifiable.

Anytime you get in a conversation about your vegan lifestyle choice, questions will no doubt be raised. You will often be mocked, laughed at, misunderstood, and ignored, but it's important to be ready for this. You can help the animals by being prepared and having all the answers to any questions people throw at you. Answering questions about things like protein, vitamin B12, and canine teeth, will give you an opportunity to sow a seed in the minds of the questioner. Hopefully that seed will sprout and as you water it with more answers and information, it will flower into a compassionate vegan mind.

Many vegans were meat eaters for years before they went vegan. Although I am ashamed to say it, I ate meat for over thirty years before making the connection and committing to helping the animals and going vegan. This is important to remember so that we don't treat meat eaters like the enemy. They are just like we were. I wish I had met a vegan who was able to give me all the answers years ago, and if I was given the information as a child, I think I would have made the connection long ago. The internet has given this opportunity to the vegan movement now, as information is easy to access and easy to spread around. The lies that have been told by the meat, egg, and dairy industries for so long, can quickly and easily be checked and revealed to be false. We can look beyond the facade of the happy chicken on the billboard or side of the delivery van, and clearly see the shameful, disgusting, and unacceptable cruelty and pain inflicted on animals everyday.

Individuals can make an immediate difference just by making the connection and deciding to not eat animals or use animals for entertainment, experimentation, clothing, or profit. As more and more individuals come together, we find ourselves in a position where we truly can change the world for the better.

CHAPTER 2

HOW TO USE THIS BOOK

"Education is the most powerful weapon which you can use to change the world."

-Nelson Mandela

This book is a go to guide that you can use when talking about your vegan lifestyle choice. If someone presents you with a question but you don't know how to answer it, then you are not helping the animals. Having the answer in your mind ready to deliver to them, will make them stop and think about what they have said and will sow that important seed.

You will find that you get asked the same few questions most of the time, with some unique ones chucked in every now and then; though not very often. I have laid out the book in sections to cover each area of questioning, including: Nature and Biology, Taste, Nutrition and Health, Environment, Farming, Vegan Myths, Morality and Behaviour, and Other. Each individual question is presented in the contents page so you can quickly find it when you need it.

I recommend really learning the most common questions and answers if you are new to Veganism. It won't take you long to figure out what they are! Then you can spend time going through all the others and building your arsenal of knowledge. It's not recommend to read through the whole book in one go like you would a novel, rather to dip in and pick out specific areas that you are interested in or that have been presented to you by friends and family.

It's really important to note that these answers are not definitive. I wrote this book to help me as much as to help you. As I was new to Veganism, I had to find out the answers from a lot of different sources. Hopefully I have saved you from doing this by compiling them all in on place and writing them in a style that suits a friendly and sensible fact based approach. You should explore them, debate them with friends, try to dismantle them or add to them, even make notes on the pages with your own thoughts. I would love to hear how you would tackle a question differently, or how you would strengthen one. If you think I have got any plain wrong, then let me know. We are always learning and although I have tried my best, it is impossible to have all the answers. It would be amazing to hear from you on our social media platforms, especially Twitter, where we hang out most of the time online. Email is great too.

Answering questions people have with logical, rational, and sensible information is key to helping the animals, and helping people to realise that Veganism is the best choice for a bright future for our children, the animals, and the planet itself. As vegans, we all know better, so I firmly believe we have to do better. Encouraging other people to know better is our first step, then we can help them to do better too.

CHAPTER 3

EXPECT HOSTILITY

"First they ignore you, then they laugh at you, then they fight you, then you win."

- Mahatma Gandhi

We need to talk to as many people as we can about being a vegan. You will probably know that conversations can go a number of ways. People can be interested and willing to learn something new, or, they can be negative, hostile and defensive. Sometimes people will have lots of questions for you, or will just ask a couple to be polite.

Talking about Vegansim is not always plain sailing. Often, people will become hostile and even aggressive, but remember, almost everyone is against animal cruelty. So if they are against it, and you tell them everything wrong with the meat, egg, fish, and dairy industries, then they have to go vegan, don't they? If they don't, they experience incongruence between what they believe and how they really act and behave. This, I believe, is the root of their hostility.

If you are aware of the idea of incongruence and expect that some people will be hostile, then you can prepare yourself to be calm when it happens. There will obviously be times when your passion will clash with their ignorance, and calmness will go out of the window, but do your best, after all, its about helping the animals, not our egos.

My wife Rachael and I have found that when we say: 'we have gone vegan because we feel it's better for our children', other parents actually hear: 'you are mistreating your children by not going vegan'. A simple and honest statement about our vegan lifestyle choice can immediately annoy some people. Others will be interested and ask us why its better, and then we have the opportunity to have a nice conversation and really explore the vegan lifestyle together. These are the best conversations to have and people can really take on the idea of Veganism quickly when they are open to new information. Don't be put off by negative reactions though, just keep calm and nice and answer the questions they give you. By the end of most conversations, people chill out a bit.

You can end the encounter by reminding the person that if they think it is wrong to inflict unnecessary pain and suffering on animals, then they already think like a vegan. That's what being a vegan is all about; leading a compassionate life, and not inflicting unnecessary pain and death on animals, while also helping the planet and benefiting our health. Who wouldn't want all those things?

CHAPTER 4

LEAVE THE TROLLS UNDER THEIR BRIDGE

"Never argue with an idiot."

- George Carlin

One thing we quickly learned was to avoid engaging with internet trolls. There is no point getting into an argument on Twitter or Facebook. It leads nowhere and we have found we only come away annoyed and wound up.

People have to be ready to make a change and they have to be open to new information and ideas. Whenever someone posts a picture of a steak or a bacon sandwich on a Vegan social media feed, you know they are not there to learn something new or engage in a rational conversation or even a debate. They are there for their own entertainment; nothing else. So we choose to avoid these trolls and don't engage. It's easy to delete a comment, block or ban them.

Not everyone will agree with this, and many feel they need to show the troll for the moron they are, and engage in long conversations online. I don't think this is wrong, but it's not the approach we have chosen. We have made the decision to not engage with faceless cowards who's only intention is to upset complete strangers for no end other than personal satisfaction and gratification. We leave them to their hate and move on to help the animals by engaging with people who are capable of talking seriously about Veganism. We don't have to convert people over night, our job is to answer their questions and sow seeds in their minds that will make them look further and hopefully make their own connection, just like we did.

CHAPTER 5

PATIENCE, PERSISTENCE, AND POSITIVITY

"Alone we can do so little; together we can do so much."

- Helen Keller

I have found that there are 3 keys to focus on to achieve a goal in business or in life, and if you are in the business of promoting Veganism and positive change, then you need to make these your new friends. They are, Patience, Persistence, and Positivity.

You have to be Patient. Not everyone is ready to change or even listen to new information. Some people will get it and make the connection right away, while others may take years. Unfortunately, some people will never listen or ever make the connection, and are too obsessed by their habits and traditions to even consider Veganism as an option. But don't be deterred. There are many people out there that want to listen and will change, so if we can keep patient then we can find these people and really make a difference to their world and that of the animals.

Persistence doesn't mean you have to nag everyone. It just means you have to keep going, no matter how difficult it gets, no matter how many rude comments and knock backs you receive. Some (probably most) people will react with dumb questions and even get defensive when you bring up Veganism, but if you keep talking about it and showing them the benefits to health, the environment, and the animals, how can they fail to see that Veganism is the best and only option for a bright future?

Remaining Positive is so important. People will try to drag you down. They will taunt you, make jokes, belittle you, even be rude and call you names. You will find people sending you pictures of bacon with quotes like 'mmm yummy' or 'I'm going to eat two steaks now instead of one.' Ignore these reactions and keep positively promoting the vegan message. While people can bring others down, we can bring them up. We can portray Veganism as the kind and compassionate movement it really is. So while it is easy to get dragged into an argument, remember, meat eaters are not our enemy, after all, most vegans probably ate meat themselves.

If we can keep calm and be positive, then we can lead by example and show others an appealing alternative way to sail through their lives with compassion at the helm. I strive to always be Patient, Persistent, and Positive, and to speak out and be the voice of the animals at every opportunity I get. This isn't fight club, this is Vegan Club, so tell everyone about Vegan Club!

CHAPTER 6

THE VEGAN SALES PROCESS

"A-B-C. A-Always, B-Be, C-Closing. Always Be Closing."

- Blake, Glengarry Glen Ross (1992)

I was listening to a talk by James Aspey , An awesome Australian guy, really chilled out, who takes the same approach to Veganism that we have. He treats everyone nicely, respectfully, and doesn't view meat eaters as enemies of vegans. Anyone who is truly compassionate will be kind to all animals, including humans! During an amazing speech he gave (link in the bibliography section), Aspey briefly touched on the idea that promoting Veganism was similar to working in sales. He pointed out that answering questions from non-vegans is just like answering objections from prospective buyers.

If you have ever worked in the sales industry, you will know that objections are reasons prospective customers give not to buy from you. Sales people treat these objections as questions and find they are asked the same ones over and

over again. A good salesperson will have all the answers
ready to hand and will practice and prepare for them. As
they receive new questions, they make a note, go away,
research and rehearse the new answers. Over time a good
salesperson will welcome objections, as each time an
objection is handled (or a question is answered) the sales
person is moving one step closer towards closing the sale.

But what does selling have to do with promoting
Veganism? Selling is all about business, the transaction of a
commodity from one entity to another. A person needs
something and another person or company can provide them
with it. This isn't just a product though, it can be a service, a
solution, or information. That's just what a book caters to. A
person requires knowledge and the author sells it to them.

This got me to thinking that just as a product or service
requires a sales process to get it into the hands or mind of the
end user, so does an idea. An idea can be sold to someone.
When we look at this, we can see it happening all around us
everyday. Convincing our children to tidy their room is an
obvious example. After owning my own business and
previously working in sales, I know how important it is to sell
ideas to staff so everyone works together. After spending
some time on the idea of selling an idea and developing a
kind of 'Vegan Sales Process', I started to get really excited
and knew I had to write a book around this concept.

Having the right answer for each objection we receive
from a non-vegan, is crucial in ensuring they leave the
conversation better informed than when they arrived. I
always aim to give sound information and encourage them to
research further by giving them links to follow up with. If we
can sow a seed in everyone we meet, imagine how many
people we would inform about Veganism over our life time?

If we don't have the answers, then what will the person leaving the conversation think and feel about Veganism? They will probably stick with their false preconceptions and carry on thinking that eating meat and animal products is good. So having all the answers, to all the objections, is crucial to do the vegan movement, and most importantly the animals, justice. If I couldn't stand up and speak for myself, how would I want someone to do it for me? I know I would want people to stand up and tell the truth, give the facts, and change the awful, horrendous situation I was in. That's how I think. I want to be the voice of these animals, and they deserve the very best I am capable of.

Now, selling isn't what you might think anymore. It's not a dodgy car salesman trying to sell you a heap of junk for a premium price. Sales needs to be ethical. The old saying, 'they could sell ice to the eskimos', is just not cool. Excuse the pun. The eskimos just don't need ice, so it's not a great thing to do to sell it to them! Same goes for the sand to Arabs. If someone doesn't want or need something, then trying to sell it to them is a waste of their time and resources, and yours.

But how does this stand for the idea of Veganism? Surely everyone doesn't want it or know they need it? Well, customers don't always know what they need. A great example of this idea is Apple. I know everyone talks about Apple, but it's for a very good reason: the company is genius. They didn't follow the old path of asking the customer what they wanted or needed and giving it to them. Instead they turned it completely on its head and asked, 'what can we provide that is better than anything else out there?' The majority of customers would not have thought they needed a tablet, a hand held device that they could operate by touching the screen. Imagine a phone without number keys on it?! Apple, on the other hand, knew this kind of technology would change how we do business, entertain ourselves, and function as modern human beings. They had an idea and used it to change the world.

So fellow Vegans, do you think we have something to sell? I think so. We know that the Vegan lifestyle is better for the animals, our health, and our planet. Now we have this knowledge should we keep it to ourselves? Is it ethical to do so? I argue that because we know better, we have to do better. We have a revolutionary product to sell that will improve the health of many people. Our product will save billions of lives every year. Our product will heal the planet and make sure the future is bright for our children and future generations to come.

What is our product? Veganism!

CHAPTER 7

NEEDS MEANS DESIRE

"The starting point of all achievement is desire."

- Napoleon Hill

There are three keys required in order to sell to anyone. These three keys were the first thing I learned in my first sales position. If your potential customer, or lead, does not need the product, have the means to pay for it, or desire it, then you don't have much chance of selling them and probably shouldn't try. But if they have one, two or even all three, they are ready to be sold and it would be rude not to sell to them! After all, you have just what they need, want, and can afford, so give it to them.

If they don't have all three, perhaps someone who eats meat is suffering bad health and they need an intervention, then the good news is that you can give them the other two. You can create desire for them based on their need. Do they want to live long enough to see their grandchildren or walk their daughter down the aisle? It could be that serious for them. In my case, I had no desire to go from a vegetarian to a vegan, after all, I thought I was doing a good thing. Until the desire presented itself in the form of a documentary called 'Earthlings'. I watched in horror at the reality of the egg and dairy industries. I saw the suffering, cruelty and all out torture the poor animals were going through and I couldn't eat another egg or piece of cheese ever again.

The desire to stop this overpowered my desire to eat pizza. This is why going vegan was very easy for me. I feel that if you have the right information and explore the areas talked about in this book, then there is no reason why 'slip ups' or 'cheats' or 'relapses' will ever be terms you will apply to your diet. Once you are completely sold on the idea of going Vegan, that purchase is for life. A meat eater may not have the desire to stop eating meat, but if you show them how destructive and cruel the meat industry is, then perhaps that desire will present itself. The desire to not torture or kill will over power the desire to fill their stomach. Desire to do good is a powerful thing, but getting there can be difficult.

Can someone need something and not know it? I believe they can. Imagine if everyone carried on eating meat and living the western life style as they are now. If China and other large developing countries adopt this lifestyle, just how bad will the world be? It's been estimated that by 2050, the oceans could be empty of life, and if the oceans die, we die. If we wipe out all the bees, then we are in serious risk of starvation. We all need to change our lifestyle to make the future viable for our children and their children. This need is huge and I think most people would agree with this.

What about means? Can anyone purchase or take on this idea of Veganism? Of course they can. Veganism is no more expensive than eating meat, and we personally find we spend a little less each week on our food shopping bills. We are not alone and many people report that this is the case. So if someone can afford to eat a meat based diet, they can afford to go vegan. No loans are required, no payment plan, the only account that will benefit is your moral one.

So now we know what our product is and how to sell it, lets begin exploring all of the objections you will face as part of the Vegan Sales Team!

SECTION 1 - NATURE & BIOLOGY

CHAPTER 8

WE ARE CARNIVORES

"I have no doubt that it is a part of the destiny of the human race, in its gradual improvement, to leave off eating animals, as surely as the savage tribes have left off eating each other...."

- Henry David Thereau

We are definitely not Carnivores, though our physiology does allow us to eat both animals and plants. We would not survive on a diet of meat alone, but interestingly, we can survive and thrive on just a plant based vegan diet. So are we Omnivores or Herbivores?

If we only ate meat then we would see deficiencies in minerals and vitamins. Fibre would not be present in any where near high enough quantities to keep our gut healthy. We would start to see many problems arising in all areas of our body and health, and eventually an early death. An interesting study found that red meat contains a sugar that our body and immune system treats as a toxin. Antibodies are produced in reaction to consumption, and this leads to inflammation on a cellular level, which is one of the causes of cancer. If we were meant to eat meat, then surely this reaction would not occur.

This is why the world health organisation (WHO) has classified processed meats – including ham, salami, sausages and hot dogs – as a class 1 carcinogen, which means that there is strong evidence that processed meats cause cancer. Red meat, such as beef, lamb and pork has been classified as a 'probable' cause of cancer. Eating meat in large quantities over a long period of time, is linked to many other diseases. Heart disease, many cancers, and diabetes are just a few of them. A great book called 'How Not To Die', by Dr Michael Greger, lists the most common causes of death and shows with very detailed evidence, the parts meat, eggs, and dairy play. We have written a short review about it on our website.

So we are in no way able to survive and thrive on a diet consisting only of meat. In short, we are not carnivores. We could not exist without eating any fruits or vegetables. A strict carnivorous diet would result in a poor experiment for mankind.

To answer the question whether we are Omnivores or Herbivores, I would say we are omnivores as we are capable of consuming both animals and plants. Does this mean we have to consume both? No. We can choose a plant based diet and thrive just as well - arguably better - as a Herbivore.

Herbivores only eat plant based foods. The largest land animals on the planet are herbivores. Elephants, hippos, even the muscular Rhino, all survive on a plant based diet. These animals are true herbivores, so meat is off the menu. As chosen and self proclaimed herbivores, vegans are able to make informed decisions about their diet and take advantage of the years of evolution to make the right decisions for their body and health.

Perhaps we couldn't survive in nature as our ancestors did without eating meat. There is a good argument for this. However, we are not our ancestors. We are a product of their sacrifice and suffering. We have used our brains to develop alternatives such as omega-3 DHA and EPA fatty acids capsules, made from algae. We can import walnuts, brazil nuts and almonds, from any where in the world. We can grow soy, flax, wheat and turn them into nutritional alternatives to meat. We can make sure we harvest a variety of vegetables and fruits and bring them altogether across the globe. We are no longer limited to our immediate surroundings and we no longer have to live like our ancestors did.

When I compared our mouth, teeth, jaw, and digestive system, to carnivores, omnivores, and herbivores, I found we were more in line with the Herbivore classification. You can see the comprehensive comparison in Appendix A.

In short, we are able to thrive on a plant based diet and can choose to be Herbivores. We don't need meat, eggs, or dairy, to survive and they are actually harming us if we are consuming them.

CHAPTER 9

WE HAVE CANINE TEETH, SO WE ARE MEANT TO EAT MEAT.

"Note that the eating of flesh is not only physically against nature, but it also makes us spiritually coarse and gross by reason of satiety and surfeit."

- Plutarch

I have covered the issue of carnivore vs herbivore in the previous chapter, but the issue of canine teeth comes up a lot, so I think it's useful to have a short chapter devoted to it. The idea that our canine teeth must mean we are meant to eat meat, is totally flawed. The comparison tables in Appendix A covers this issue but there are a few points to highlight in addition to it.

Our canine teeth are nothing like those of a tiger, shark, or even a dog. Our whole jaw, skeleton, muscles, and digestive system are more in line with herbivores. Even if we had massive canine teeth, it would be no indicator that we are 'meant' to be eating meat. In fact, the animal with the largest canine teeth is actually the Hippo! Hippos are completely, 100%, herbivorous and use their huge teeth - and head - to defend themselves.

There is a famous proposal by the author Harvey Diamond who suggested, "You put a baby in a crib with an apple and a rabbit. If it eats the rabbit and plays with the apple, I'll buy you a new car." There are a couple of flaws here. You could put a rabbit and apple with a puppy, a tiger cub, maybe even a wolf cub, and they probably wouldn't eat either of the two. A baby wouldn't be able to eat the apple anyway. But he might be on to something. If you presented a grown up, fully developed adult human with an apple and a live rabbit, the grown up would obviously eat the apple. They would no doubt find the rabbit to be cute and cuddly and want to cuddle it. Now give the apple and rabbit to an adult wolf, dog, or tiger. The wild animals would tear that rabbit up and the apple would be pushed aside. Even some domestic dogs would eat the rabbit. Obviously some wouldn't. My Alfie dog, a golden labrador, would not harm it and in fact we used to have a house rabbit that would boss him around. Plus he loves apples!

My point here is that just because we have canine teeth, doesn't mean we are inclined to, or meant to, eat meat. Our instinct is not to kill and eat live animals if other foods are available. Popping to the supermarket and buying a vacuum packed plastic tray of meat is totally different. This is so far detached from the reality or catching and killing a live animal that has to be plucked, skinned, gutted and cut up. Most meats have to be cooked and I don't see many obligate carnivores doing this.

When people say it's natural to eat meat, they have no idea what it would be like to naturally hunt, catch, kill, skin, gut, bleed out, and cut up an animal. It's not natural to go to the supermarket and buy something that is so far removed from an animal as possible, like chicken nuggets, fish fingers, or a lasagne. Swap the processed, reformed, and cooked meat products for a pigs head, and then see what comes naturally.

CHAPTER 10

WE HAVE EVOLVED TO EAT MEAT

"If you declare that you are naturally designed for such a diet, then first kill for yourself what you want to eat. Do it, however, only through your own resources, unaided by cleaver or cudgel or any kind of ax."

- Plutarch

If you had to choose an animal to be in a small room with and fight them to the death so you could eat them, what animal would be at the edge of your capability to overpower and eat? All you have are your bare hands, no tools, traps or weapons, and no cooking devices.

A squirrel, mouse or rat, would be so difficult to catch, and even if you caught them, could you safely eat them raw? Why does the thought of eating them raw make you feel sick? I argue it's because it is just not natural. Any other natural predator of these animals would have no problem catching and eating them, guts and all.

What about a house cat? Do you think they would put up a fight? They would go crazy, scratching, biting, inflicting small injuries on you. Yes, I'm sure I could kill a cat, but again, eating them raw? Then how would I treat my wounds, would they become infected? Not having a tough skin or hair as protection, would leave me easily susceptible to wounds.

Once we go bigger than this, a pig, cow, horse, or sheep, how do we catch and kill them? A headlock might do the trick, strangle them to death maybe, or rip out their throat with our mouth and teeth. But then what? We would have to get through thick skin, hair, and fleece. We would have to chew through the tough tendons and muscles, knowing on bone while the blood ran out from the trembling, dead corpse we would find ourselves presented with. The animal would not give in without a fight, and their teeth, hooves, and sheer mass, would no doubt cause us some problems.

These are all just prey animals. What happens when we come face to face with a predator? A wolf, tiger, hippo, crocodile, or hyena? We wouldn't stand a chance. Their instinct is to kill, tear out our throats and even eat us when we are still alive. Our natural instincts are to avoid such a fight, and we are certainly not physically equipped to take on such a beast.

But you might say, 'well, we developed tools, hunted in packs, used our brains to overpower and outwit the animals'. And this brings me to my point. If we can use our brains to eat the animals, then we can use our brains to not eat them. We can learn about nutrition and health. We can develop alternatives that give us everything meat does but without the cruelty to the animals or loss of life, and remove the many negative health effects too. In short, we can learn to be Vegan!

So when someone says to me, 'we evolved to eat meat', I say, yes but then we evolved further so as not to eat it!

We don't crave a dead, bleeding, hairy, writhing animal when we are hungry. We do crave sugar, fruit, fatty foods rich in carbohydrates. If we had evolved to eat meat, do you think we would look differently? Would we be faster not slower? Would we be walking upright or on all fours? Would we be able to eat raw chicken without risk of disease, or would be able to digest it quickly to prevent this? Would our teeth and jaw be more like those of a dog or wild cat? Would we be physically stronger, with a tougher skin?

The argument to eat meat based on our evolution is just crazy. It is so obvious that we have either evolved to not eat meat, or have never been able to eat it at all. If you are still unsure if you have evolved to eat meat, just ask yourself which would you prefer, a nice piece of fruit or a dead, hairy, bloody rat?

If anything, we have evolved to eat meat infrequently as opportunistic hunter gatherers. Perhaps eating meat only once or twice per month. This is why tribes give such value to the liver of their catch and allow the highest ranking individuals the privilege of eating it first. We see this in wolf packs too, with the Alpha getting the first choice of the spoils. The liver is packed with nutrients, so this would top up a diet of foraged fruit and vegetable and starchy foods such as tapioca. This is shown in some hunter gatherer tribes that still exist today.

They will hunt or even take the remains of a kill made by another animal. In Africa there is a tribe that live in the same area as lions who take advantage of the lions kill to bring home meat for their family. Carefully moving in, they will work as a team to get close to the carcass and remove some of it before carefully backing away. They will only take a portion of the kill, perhaps a leg, and leave the rest to the lions. Working with nature, rather than against it. They haven't evolved to kill the animal themselves, they have evolved to use their brain power so they just don't have to. And this is just like us inventing tofu, seitan, and other meat substitutes. Do you think this tribe would risk death by lion attack if they could just pop up the trail and buy some pre prepared, safe to eat, nutritious and healthy meat substitute? Of course they would choose the meat substitute, and so would most of us if given the choice.

CHAPTER 11

IT'S TRADITION

"In an earlier stage of our development most human groups held to a tribal ethic. Members of the tribe were protected, but people of other tribes could be robbed or killed as one pleased. Gradually the circle of protection expanded, but as recently as 150 years ago we did not include blacks. So African human beings could be captured, shipped to America and sold. In Australia white settlers regarded Aborigines as a pest and hunted them down, much as kangaroos are hunted down today. Just as we have progressed beyond the blatantly racist ethic of the era of slavery and colonialism, so we must now progress beyond the speciesist ethic of the era of factory farming, of the use of animals as mere research tools, of whaling, seal hunting, kangaroo slaughter and the destruction of wilderness. We must take the final step in expanding the circle of ethics."

- Peter Singer

The English Sunday Roast, Turkey for Christmas Dinner or Thanksgiving. A hotdog or pie at the big game. These are all things we have grown up with and no doubt enjoyed at some part of our lives. Once you become vegan, you realise all these things are unnecessary. You can enjoy a vegan roast dinner with gravy and all the trimmings, vegan hotdogs and pies too! So although meat is given pride of place at the centre of our most cherished family get togethers, it really doesn't have to be at the cost of an animals life anymore.

Imagine a Christmas meal where no animal has had to die just for you to over eat? You can all sit around laughing and joking, loving and sharing, but over a tofurkey rather than the corpse of a real one.

Tradition can still be tradition without the meat sacrifice. These special occasions are all about who you spend them with so it really doesn't matter that you don't eat anyone during them. In fact, the idea of not killing an animal when you don't have to should add to the celebration. And what's wrong with starting a new tradition? In our house this christmas we will celebrate with every single vegetable you can imagine! Our table will be a feast of delicious, vibrant, healthy foods, with no sacrifice or murder included.

I like to think about traditions, such as a turkey at christmas, as something I used to do as a child. I don't think back and hate my parents for not being vegan. Or course not. They were giving me turkey because they thought I needed meat, just as I gave my daughter meat when she was younger. As with the section on 'we have always eaten meat', just because we have always done something, doesn't mean we should continue to do it. Old traditions can be maintained and celebrated with new alternative methods. We can honour the past while honouring the living, and make sure we don't carry on the slaughter just because our ancestors who didn't know any better did.

CHAPTER 12

LARGE BRAINS BECAUSE OF EATING MEAT

"It is just like mans vanity and impertinence to call an animal dumb because it is dumb to his dull perceptions."

- Mark Twain

Just because we have always done bad, doesn't mean we have to continue to. Things change, opinions change, people change. Slavery in America only ended in 1860 and up until quite recently, black people couldn't sit next white people on a bus, or frequent the same bars and clubs, drink from the same water fountain, or even use the same toilets. We figured out that slavery was bad and we put a stop to it. Our immoral behaviour in the past does not support continuous bad behaviour today.

The same goes for eating meat and producing eggs and dairy. Just because we have always done this, doesn't mean we always have to. In fact, we seem to be getting worse. The way we factory farm now is terrible for the animals. Instead of driving them across the plains, we are confining them in tiny spaces, feeding them processed foods, pumping them with antibiotics and chemicals, and creating enormous lakes of their waste that pollutes the surrounding environment. Instead of realising what we have done is wrong, we are scaling up the pain and torture on an incredible level. As the worlds population passes seven billion, and developing countries look to the West for how to live, the factory farming and animal slaughter is increasing.

Our large, developed brain may be great at figuring out how to calculate complicated equations, build giant buildings, and fly us through space, but when it comes to ethics and morality, at times we are retarded.

Many reports suggest meat was not the key player in our brain development anyway. But even if it can be shown that we have evolved to our present state because we ate meat, it doesn't mean we should carrying on doing it. Eating meat now is not going to make our brains any bigger or better. In fact, eating meat is harming our bodies.

If eating meat results in larger and more developed brains, then why aren't obligate carnivores like lions and hyenas the most intelligent animals the planet? Why aren't their brains much bigger and why aren't they writing books about the benefits of eating meat?

Shouldn't we use these large brains that we find ourselves with to do better? We must take what we have learned and use it to stop the unnecessary harm of animals. We know what is right and wrong, good and bad. We just have to face the reality and do the right thing for the animals, ourselves, and the planet.

CHAPTER 13

TOP OF THE FOOD CHAIN

"The animals you eat are not those who devour others; you do not eat the carnivorous beasts, you take them as your pattern. You only hunger for the sweet and gentle creatures which harm no one, which follow you, serve you, and are devoured by you as the reward of their service."

- Jean-Jacques Rousseau

When I think of the top of the food chain, I think of the Great White Shark, A lion, or a crocodile. Put me out in the wilderness with no weapons or tools, and I don't know how long I would last. Make that wilderness in Africa or the Amazon jungle, and the odds of survival tip well out of my favour. We are no more at the top of the food chain than an otter. Does anyone really think they could overpower a shark, lion, or crocodile on their own, one on one, with no tools or weapons? Wouldn't it be easier to pick some apples, or dig up some roots vegetables? The answer is obvious.

Humans are lucky because we can choose what we eat. We go into this in detail in the sections on Teeth and Carnivores.

This choice had made us believe we are great predators because on the most part, we have chosen to eat meat. We have chosen to tame and domesticate entire species just so we can breed them for our food. This doesn't make us a predator, this makes us a master of edible slaves.

We are definitely not top of our self constructed food chain. Instead, we have removed ourselves from the chain altogether, and used our advancements in tools and technology to gradually manipulate and enslave nature. Rather than co-exist with animals and our planet, we have chosen to rape and dominate them. Choosing a plant based vegan diet will stop this happening.

It's obvious that when we make the comparison to a real Apex predator, humans do not rate closely to them at all. The fact that we can use our brains to effectively hunt and overpower these creatures, does not give us license to do so. We can use our brains to positions ourselves on the top of a different chain; the moral one.

CHAPTER 14

WE HAVE ALWAYS EATEN ANIMALS, SINCE PREHISTORIC TIMES

"The thinking [person] must oppose all cruel customs no matter how deeply rooted in tradition and surrounded by a halo. When we have a choice, we must avoid bringing torment and injury into the life of another..."

- Albert Schweitzer

Technology has removed our need to hunt and eat meat. The world we live in is very different than the one our ancestors experienced and we certainly have more options available to us. We can farm and harvest on grand scales and replace anything we might have got from meat with plant based alternatives. We no longer have to eat meat, eggs, or dairy to survive. It is easy to survive and thrive on a vegan plant based diet.

We live in an amazing time. Technology has advanced us in so many ways. If we embrace the good that technology brings, then we can transcend this backwards way of thinking and move forward towards a brighter future, free of cruelty and unnecessary suffering. The only reasons to carry on eating meat, eggs, and dairy are selfish taste, lazy convenience, stubborn tradition, and ignorance.

If anyone still wants to look back to what our prehistoric ancestors did to justify eating meat today, then shouldn't they also look at other behaviours? Cannibalism, Rape, Murder, Slavery, Sacrifice. Are these traditions we want to be adhering to? Eating meat because our prehistoric ancestors did, is just like throwing our kids in to a volcano to make the sun rise again. Just because an ancient civilisation believed it, doesn't mean we have to repeat it. We can see they were wrong on so many levels, and if we can all make the same connection where animals are concerned, then the world will be a better place.

Societies learn and evolve. Some things that were acceptable at one stage in our history are not acceptable now. One day eating meat will be one of those things too.

Choosing one behaviour from the past to justify our behaviour now, while at the same time ignoring the rest, is not a good enough argument. If anyone truly believes we should eat meat because our ancestors did, then they should hunt that meat themselves. Wear the skin, move into a cave, and throw away any and all possessions and technologies that our ancestors wouldn't have had. This sounds ridiculous, but no more so than eating meat just because cavemen did. Sometimes to show how absurd an argument is, you just have to turn it around and indulge in the absurdity yourself.

CHAPTER 15

EATING ANIMALS IS INSTINCTUAL

"Very little of the great cruelty shown by men can really be attributed to cruel instinct. Most of it comes from thoughtlessness or inherited habit. The roots of cruelty, therefore, are not so much strong as widespread. But the time must come when inhumanity protected by custom and thoughtlessness will succumb before humanity championed by thought. Let us work that this time may come."

- Albert Schwetizer

Doing something because it seems instinctual, doesn't make it right. As a society, we have learned that murder, rape, physical violence, and theft are all immoral acts. At one time, these things were instinctual, and to some, they still are. Most people have repressed these instincts and can tell the difference between right and wrong. They can stop themselves indulging in instinctual pleasures if these pleasures affect other people.

At one time in my life, I used to think it was an instinctual act to eat animals, and I didn't think anyone was harmed by it. I am ashamed to say that I didn't think of the animals as anyone, only as a 'thing'. I love to camp out in the woods, build a fire and I used to enjoy cooking meat over it. It felt good to be out in nature. But if I had to catch and kill that meat instead of picking it up from a shop on my way to camp, my experience would have been very different. I certainly wouldn't have been relaxing on my sleeping mat, or sitting on a log. I would be out stalking in the woods, setting traps, and trying anything I could to get my meal. Meanwhile, whoever I was with would be scavenging for berries, fruits, nuts, and vegetables. It wouldn't be such a relaxing time, but would be much more like the experience our ancestors would have had. If our instincts guide us to eat meat, then surely they should be guiding us to hunt it, rather than buy it in neat little packages, trimmed and prepared, seasoned and flavoured?

When I really sat and thought about it, I quickly realised my instinct is actually not to eat meat. The more time I spend with animals the less I want to kill and eat them. The more vegetables and fruit I eat, the more I enjoy them and want to eat more. I know we went through this earlier, but a lot of the arguments over lap. Have a look at the rabbit vs apple scenario in the chapter on Canine Teeth to see if instinct would drive an adult human to favour a live rabbit over a crisp apple.

I'm sure that if I was starving, my instincts would be to eat anything that I can find, but, just like the Desert Island scenario, I am not starving. I am not in some fictitious situation where I have to choose between eating an animal - or even a person - or death.

But what about natural urges? The urge to kill, rape, and steal, are these instincts too? Or are they just remnants of a primitive time? We can tell what is right and wrong, and I strive to be a good and decent human being. I'm pretty sure everyone gets an unusual urge of some kind every now and then, but we have learned to resist such an urge and do the right thing instead. If we treat the eating of meat as instinctual, then are we secretly allowing ourselves to act on our other urges too?

Imagine a world where a few generations have come through believing that we shouldn't eat meat, abuse animals, or destroy our environment. Imagine if most people were Vegans, and only a small percentage of people ate meat. Our instinct would really be to be vegan wouldn't it? Any time a minority emerges, they are treated as outcasts, weirdos, cults, or worse, religious! But over time, minorities can grow and grow until they are the general concensus of a civilisation.

Would you rather a world full of people who don't harm animals or a world full of people that do? Would you rather define yourself as an instinctual, spontaneous, reactive individual, or a rational, thinking, progressive one? I know which I would choose.

CHAPTER 16

ANIMALS EAT ANIMALS

"A man can live and be healthy without killing animals for food; therefore, if he eats meat, he participates in taking animal life merely for the sake of his appetite. And to act so is immoral."

- Leo Tolstoy

It seems a bit odd to even address such an objection, but it comes up from time to time, so it's in the book! The obvious response to this is "so should we do everything that animals do?" If we advocate one animalistic behaviour, then shouldn't we advocate them all? I went into detail on this idea in the Lions Eat Meat Section.

We do far more things that animals don't do, yet we think we should use animals as examples of how we should eat? This is an outdated and unnecessary mindset.

Many animals don't even eat meat, so why should we be led by the ones that do? If I had to choose which animal to behave like, I would probably choose a Gorilla over a Lion. I could sit around eating vegetables and fruit, maybe the odd insect, but at least I wouldn't have to chase down a gazelle and rip it apart with my teeth and claws, eating parts of it while it died slowly beneath my hot sweaty body.

If we do want to explore the comparison between how we kill animals and how animals kill animals, then we can go there too. Animals in nature kill what they need to eat. They may also kill to defend their family or to stop other animals moving into their territory and hunting grounds. Most animals, most of the time, will only kill what they need to in order to survive.

Humans, on the other hand, take things to a whole new level. We breed animals and act like we care for them. We keep them confined and feed them unnatural foods packed with hormones and antibiotics. When we kill them, we do it in a production line using tools, before cutting them up into neat packages or mincing them until they are unrecognisable. One further awful aspect of the meat industry and our lust for meat and poultry, is the amount of meat that is wasted. It is estimated that 20% of all meat and poultry is wasted, just thrown away. This is disgusting; 20% of all animals deaths are for absolutely nothing.

You may be aware of the old, 'foxes kill for fun' retort. Foxes will kill all the chickens they find and leave them where they lay, not for the sake of killing, but to come back for them later. After all, they can only carry so many back to their den in one go. This is a common misconception, and farmers will often express their disgust for foxes and their 'murderous' behaviour. The farmers obviously leave out the bit about imprisoning animals in small cages, artificially impregnating them, killing off male chicks with death by gas, suffocation, or grinding machine. If the farmers left the dead chickens, the fox would return to eat them. They just see an opportunity and kill everything they find. Not for the sake of killing, but to take advantage of an opportunity to feed their family well.

It is a crazy idea that because some animals eat animals, and we are animals too, we should indulge in the same behaviour. Eating other animals because some animals eat other animals is a flawed argument for many reasons. Doing something because someone else does is no way to go about your life. Murderers murder, so we should murder. Rapists rape, so we should rape. You get the idea, and I'm sure you can think of lots of examples yourself.

If we are the most intellectual animals on the planet, as we believe we are, then we are obligated to do the right thing by all the other animals, not rule over them like some crazed flesh hungry dictatorship.

CHAPTER 17

NATURAL CIRCLE OF LIFE

"Non-violence leads to the highest ethics, which is the goal of all evolution. Until we stop harming all other living beings, we are all still savages."

- Thomas A Edison

The Natural Circle of Life Argument is very similar to arguments on evolution, lions, and other animals eating animals arguments. The slight difference that we can go into a little detail here with is that the circle of life that the animals being slaughtered in numbers over 150 billion each year, is not a natural circle.

Confining animals under factory farming conditions denies all natural behaviours. Turkeys can't even breed naturally as their breasts are so big now due to our selective breeding and over feeding.

Breaking down the factory farm process, we quickly see there is nothing natural about it. Animals are kept inside for their entire life. They have no access to grazing land and are instead fed a cocktail of antibiotics, hormones, and steroids. They have their teeth, tails, testicles, and ears cut, snipped, trimmed, and pierced. They are artificially impregnated, which is just a polite way of saying raped. Their sex decides how they will be treated. The young are torn away from the mother and either killed at a young age or put to work to produce milk or eggs, before finally being killed for cheap meat. They even have the date of their death decided for them. This is not natural.

Hunting animals because we needed to eat them to survive is totally different to breeding them on such a gross scale. The biggest insult, and perhaps the most unnatural part, is that a shocking 20% of all the animals killed, do not even get eaten. Their body parts are thrown away because they go out of date or because someone was too full to finish their meal. In nature it is rare for anything to go to waste, and the scale with which animals are killed and wasted for pure gluttony is an embarrassment of the human race.

The processes we employ to be able to produce meat, eggs, and dairy, are so far from nature that we have completely removed the idea that the meat we eat is even an animals flesh. If we can reconnect the reality of what we are doing to these innocent and peaceful animals, then I hope we can break this completely unnatural circle an do away with this outdated and absurd argument.

CHAPTER 18

LIONS EAT MEAT

"It is necessary to correct the error that vegetarianism has made us weak in mind, or passive or inert in action. I do not regard flesh-food as necessary at any stage."

- Mohanda Ghandi

I hear this one a lot. 'Lions eat meat, and they are at the top of the food chain. We are predators just like them, so we should eat meat too!'

On this rational, I have to ask, should we do everything lions do? Maybe we should act like other predators too? Should we start rolling around in other animals poo so we can tell our family all about it? Or perhaps we should start running around the Savannah and pouncing on Wilderbeast, tearing them apart with our teeth and nails.

What about other animals, we should be able to compare ourselves to them too? Surely we should be acting as they do in the wild as well. No need for law anymore, let's just fight for power and kill anyone who steps up to question our authority. We should be just like ducks and other wild fowl, and gang rape any females that take our fancy.

Let's start living and sleeping under trees, in caves or in the woods. What about toilets? We shouldn't be using them anymore, let's just dig a shallow hole and poo in that like badgers do. We don't need beds and duvets anymore, look at all these leaves lying around, let's make some bedding out of those. I'm sure our hair will grow longer during the winter months to keep us warm anyway.

Lions don't use iPhones, so let's get rid of those while we are at it. Clothes? Why bother, after all elephants don't need them. Showers? No thanks, I am going to lick myself clean from now on, and if I can't reach some part of my body? Don't worry, I'll ask someone else to get it for me, I'm sure they wont mind.

Do you remember the last time you saw a lion stop hunting wild animals and instead start to breed them in a farm environment? Build a fence around an area and keep animals in there giving them enough time to breed and reproduce before killing any. Then taking them, still alive, in lorries they figured out how to build, to an abattoir where they killed them with sharp knives they somehow learned to make with advanced blacksmith skills. Then they minced up the worst parts and open a McLions takeaway and built drive throughs so they didn't need to run anymore. Just hop in a car invented by a lion equivalent of Mr Ford (Mr Roared), and drive on down 24 hours a day for a McAntelope Burger, finished with a perfectly baked bun, baked by baker lions, and topped with crisp lettuce and sauce, grown by those resourceful farmer lions.

It's a joke to suggest we are anything like a lion (or any animal for that matter) and that we should do one thing just because they do. We have developed our brains and have been able to evolve to this point just because we don't have to hunt animals anymore. We have learned to breed them in factory farms and reduce the danger involved in eating them. But I suggest we have gone one step further, and eliminated the need to eat meat at all.

Now even if you go along with someone who says they eat meat because Lions eat meat, then what would their answer be if you asked them why they eat cheese or tomato ketchup?

So let's forget this macho, childish idea that we are apex predators that need to hunt to be a man, or that we need to eat meat because it's natural or because we have evolved to do so. If the way we treat this planet is any indication of how we have evolved to eat meat, then we have to stop right now. We can't keep destroying everything around us just to satisfy our outdated lust for meat.

If we do carry on regardless, what future will face our children and their children after them? There just may not be one, and I worry about this. Eating meat is destroying our planet, and if we keep promoting the idea as the way forward for the developing countries, then there won't be enough land available to feed their meat hunger. Then what will happen? Will this lead to war over land? Wars over animals? Come on, wake up, and see that meat is not the way forward. We don't need it. It's cruel, it's actually bad for us, and it's bad for our planet. Do people really think all of those things are less important than the desire for a good steak or bucket of chicken, some of which they will just throw away once their glutony is satisfied?

SECTION 2 - TASTE

CHAPTER 19

WHY DO ANIMALS TASTE SO GOOD?

"But for the sake of some little mouthful of meat, we deprive a soul of the sun and light, and of that proportion of life and time it had been born into the world to enjoy."

- Hippocrates

I trained as a professional Chef with the Royal Navy and so can make pretty much anything taste good with the right balance of flavourings and seasonings. Meat on it's own is often quote bland, and certainly needs a little salt to 'bring out the flavours'. I could take some road kill and turn it into an unrecognizable dish that tastes great. So if taste is a good justification to carry on murdering billions of animals every year, then surely anything that tasted good should be eaten?

Human meat is reported to taste just like pig meat, so should that be on the menu? After all, most people love bacon! I am sure the Chinese love the dog meat they eat during the Yulin Festival, yet most people in the UK think it's a disgrace and will say so while at the same time eating a pig!

The same people that say stupid things like this most probably have a pet of their own that would taste awesome if it was covered in KFC coating and deep fried, yet there seems to be a boundary they are not willing to cross, even when taste is actually concerned.

So we could accuse them of Speciesism. Favouring one species over another and applying totally different rules to how they should be treated. Eat one, sleep with another. Murder one, dress another in stupid clothes and post photos of it on Instagram professing your love for animals. Love nature and the wild creatures, but dance around a fire whilst wearing the skin of one animal and eating another.

Unfortunately, although this is a stupid argument, it is an honest one. Taste is to blame for so much animal cruelty. People are literally addicted to cheese and bacon, and fast food takeaways provide cheap, convenient, and appealing food. It was easy for me to stop eating any animal products once I knew what was involved. When I knew that free range meant nothing good for the animals, taste was easy to overcome. But it may not be as easy for everyone, especially if the connection they make is not a solid one.

When we all went vegan as a family, my wife, daughter, and I found it easy. We had all watched Earthlings and other videos and documentaries so we saw the reality and the horror. My little boy was too young at 5 years old to watch them, and he was the one that found it difficult to not have meat, eggs, milk, and cheese anymore. We persisted, 100% committed to never bring those products into our home again, but when he went to parties or friends houses, we left the choice up to him. He happily ate meat, eggs, and dairy when he could choose it but after a couple of months he noticed he would get a bad tummy after eating them. This put him off a bit. Then we came across an age appropriate cartoon in the style of 'draw my life'. It was all about a cow and the things that happen to her in the dairy industry. This put him right off milk and cheese and he won't eat it any more. This was his choice, based on the information he received in a media he could relate to and understand.

This is the key. People have to receive the information in a way that they can consume it. They may make the decision over night, which is awesome, or they may need to be drip fed and make little connections over time. I feel it is our responsibility as Vegans to drip feed this information and encourage others to go vegan. We can live our lives as an example of what is good and just and hope others will follow and adopt the vegan lifestyle too.

CHAPTER 20

I LIKE MEAT

"We need a boundless ethics which will include animals also."

- Albert Schweitzer

This is a really difficult argument for me. I used to love meat! I ate medium rare steaks, lamb chops, sausage, bacon, chicken, you name it, I was a big meat eater. One time I even ate raw liver to experience what it would be like after watching a survival programme. Writing this, I can't believe just how much I loved meat, I was even a professional chef for part of my life, cooking so much meat and poultry. Although I feel incredibly ashamed and guilty for this, it helps me remember that it can be difficult to go from a meat lover to a vegan or even to a vegetarian.

The main reason I went vegetarian was because I just didn't want to take a life if I didn't need to. I remember parking behind a meat delivery lorry outside my local butchers and seeing the pigs and lamb hanging on hooks in the back as the driver unloaded the dead animals. It made me think of how my dog, Alfie, stretched out when he liked to have his tummy rubbed. Legs stretched, fur and skin tightened across his ribs, with his pink tummy facing up. Looking at those dead animals made something click in my mind and I decided to stop eating animals straight away. I never went further than that though. I still ate eggs, cheese and dairy no problem, and actually thought I was doing good. I thought those things were doing me good too. I was so very wrong.

So meat does taste great when it's seasoned, flavoured and cooked well. There is no denying it. This argument, 'I like meat', is purely based on personal taste and pleasure. Is the suffering and gruesome death of an animal worth the pleasure in your mouth, not to mention the harm it does to your body?

I like to ask three questions:

1. Do you like harming animals?
2. Would you ever purposefully inflict harm on an animal?
3. Then why do you pay other people to kill animals so you can eat them?

Eating meat, eggs, or dairy, is cruel to the animals. This is not my opinion, this is undeniable truth. The only way you can avoid purposefully hurting animals, is to stop eating them. By eating animals, you are giving someone your permission to artificially breed, confine, quickly fatten up, and eventually violently kill them at a young age. You are giving permission to treat a life as a commodity.

You will no doubt have had someone say to you, 'ooh bacon, I could never give that up,' or 'I love a nice juicy steak.' The idea that meat is something to 'give up' is troubling. The only thing given up for the meat to be eaten is the poor animals life. That life was taken against their will, the poor animal was forced to give up their life for our plate. That animal wanted to live above all else. You chose for the animal to die just so you could have a bacon sandwich or a juicy steak. Some people even say, 'still mooing,' when they talk about a rare steak. It's so funny to them, and although they are referring to the animal, they are not making the connection between that rare steak and the cow that had their throat slit and their body dragged up in to the air with a hook through their leg, still alive, writhing in pain and full of fear and absolute terror. Their leg dislocated, broken or breaking under their own weight as their blood slowly drained out beneath them along the conveyor belt. Another cow in front, one more following it behind, witnessing the ordeal and smelling the horrific odour of death and fear. No meal is worth this.

This short simple statement sums it up for me; nothing tastes as good as vegan feels.

CHAPTER 21

I DON'T LIKE VEGETABLES

"Alas, what wickedness to swallow flesh into our own flesh, to fatten our greedy bodies by cramming in other bodies, to have one living creature fed by the death of another! In the midst of such wealth as earth, the best of mothers, provides, yet nothing satisfies you, but to behave like the Cyclopes, inflicting sorry wounds with cruel teeth! You cannot appease the hungry cravings of your wicked, gluttonous stomachs except by destroying some other life."

- Pythagoras

It's difficult being brought up your whole life eating meat products. I know, I was too. But imagine eating a burger without the tomato ketchup, the onions, the mustard, even the gherkins? These toppings give so much flavour to the burger and are all vegetables. Even the cheese slices are made with vegetable oils and the bun is flour from a plant. And what about those french fries and onion rings? Both vegetables!

I get that some people eat plain burgers, but the truth is that vegetables provide a huge part of the flavours and make up of meat products and recipes. In the UK, spaghetti Bolognese is a big favourite for family meal times. The way it is typically made there is with minced (or ground) beef, stock, onions, tomatoes from a tin, garlic, tomato puree and some herbs. Jars of sauce are very popular too, but they all contain the non meat ingredients. This meal is full of flavour from the vegetables. The beef is not necessary and just adds texture and maybe colour. Removing it completely from the recipe and replacing beef stock with a good vegetable stock, will give you a delicious and much healthier meal that is, of course, cruelty free. If you miss the meaty aspect of the dish, then add some soya mince. This stuff is great and really easy to prepare. We buy the dehydrated pure 100% soya that only needs rehydrating and adding to a sauce at the end rather than frying it as you would do with meat. You get the texture and feel of meat, with all the healthy benefits and none of the negatives.

If you don't like vegetables, and are not eating them, then you may not be in good health. Where are you getting your fibre? I think that if you really look at your diet, you will discover you are eating a lot more vegetables than you think.

There are many Vegan options available to replace the meat products. Burgers, chicken, sausages, even bacon, can all be bought in Vegan alternatives completely plant based but with the look and feel of meat. Now this is never going to be just like meat, but it is close and getting better all the time. I have recently discovered sliced vegan chicken and ham alternatives that taste exactly like luncheon meat or chicken roll does. Rather than being made up of lips, eye lids, hooves, fat, bum holes and other parts, these vegan processed style meats are made with soy, olives, and good old vegetables. If you experiment and try lots of alternatives, you will definitely find something you like. Personally, I don't like to buy the meat alternatives as I am completely put off eating meat and don't want anything to look like it. I have found some Linda McCartney sausage rolls though, that are 100% vegan and delicious, so I eat those no problem!

I found that once I had made the connection and couldn't eat meat anymore, I was encouraged to eat other fruits and vegetables that I wasn't bothered about before. We only really ate broccoli as a side with a roast dinner, but now I love it! I can't get enough broccoli and actually look forward to sitting down to a whole broccoli cooked in the wok or oven with olive oil, chilli, and garlic, sprinkled with pink Himalayan salt. Seriously, I can't believe how much I love broccoli, and other vegetables like avocado, asparagus and recently butternut squash. Now I think about broccoli as I used to think about cheeseburgers. It seems weird to say it, even now, but it's true. I even got annoyed when my local shop had sold out of broccoli recently!

The best advice is be creative and give a variety of fruits and vegetables a try. The more things you try, the more things you will like. My wife and I swear that food actually tastes better now, and the flavours in vegetables are much more pronounced. We have been having a great time experimenting and tasting a wide range of fruit and vegetables, so give it a try, I'm sure you will be pleasantly surprised.

Vegans put the animals lives above their tastebuds. This is the biggest reason that vegans are vegans; it's for the animals. So I encourage meat eaters to not let their history of vegetables put up a barrier between them and a vegan lifestyle.

SECTION 3 - NUTRITION & HEALTH

CHAPTER 22

VEGANS ARE UNHEALTHY

"He who has health, has hope; and he who has hope, has everything."

- Arabian Proverb

Being told that you are unhealthy by someone that eats flesh and organs from another animal, congealed excretion from another's breast, and a chickens period, is sometimes difficult to listen to. I just have to remember that I once did all of those things too. It is so gross to imagine that now and when I look back on how I used to eat, I do feel physically sick.

The biggest killers of humans are Heart Disease, Cancers, Diabetes, and Obesity, all of which have direct links to bad diet caused by eating meat and animal products. People don't die from eating a varied and balanced plant based diet. That is fact, pure and simple fact.

People will pick up on an anecdote they've heard about one vegan in 20 years having a B12 deficiency and they bring it up all the time. Yet they never seem to mention the millions of people that die every year because of a meat and dairy based standard western diet. For some reason, adopting in a vegan diet is more extreme than eating dead animals and their by products to such a degree that the cholesterol builds up in your arteries, resulting in you having to have your chest literally cut and sawn apart so that your arteries can have the build up of animal fats scraped out. Given the choice, most would still choose the latter.

Vegans can easily counter the arguments for B12, Protein, Calcium, Iron, and whatever else is thrown at us. You can read sections on all of these in this book, and see they are easily addressed. You do need to spend a little time planning your plant based diet, but as long as you do, you can be super healthy and reduce your risk of all the major killers of humans in our modern world. In fact, the B12 deficiency is more common in meat eaters than vegans, and B12 is given to animals as supplements and put into cows milk to fortify it. So meat eaters are getting B12 from similar sources as vegans, they just let the animals take the supplements for them!

Vegans don't have all the antibiotics that milk and meat is pumped full of either, or any of the terrible side effects or risks during pregnancy. Plant based foods are not high risk like eggs, meat, and dairy.

Of course, vegans can be unhealthy if they live on a fast food diet, consuming french fries and processed foods. But if a vegan eats a well balanced, plant based diet that meets their caloric needs, they will no doubt consume all the minerals, vitamins, nutrients, fats, carbs, and proteins they need, while filling in the well known gaps with easily purchased supplements and fortified foods.

We just don't need to eat animals to survive anymore and we can easily survive and thrive on a vegan plant based diet whilst removing all cruelty, suffering, pain, and death from our diets. We can make ourselves healthier, our children healthier, save the animals, and save the planet. Why would anyone not want to do any of these things?

CHAPTER 23

VEGANS GET ILL ALL THE TIME

"The food you eat can be either the safest and most powerful form of medicine, or the slowest form of poison."

- Ann Wigmore

I used to think being a Vegan was unhealthy too. I thought it was weird to only eat fruits and vegetables and that vegans were all skinny and extreme hippies. I never thought about all the meat eaters and the meat related illnesses such as heart disease, high blood pressure, obesity, cancer, and diabetes. When I started to research what it really meant to be a Vegan, I soon found out that it was really good for you and far healthier than a standard western diet. I couldn't believe how I had been so wrong for so long.

I found that you could get all your nutrients, vitamins, and minerals from plant based foods, and could easily supplement or eat fortified foods for your vitamins B12 and

D. Iron, protein, amino acids, and everything you can think of can be found in nuts, fruits, and vegetables. The great news was that all the bad things like saturated fats and cholesterol were left out!

Of course, Vegans can eat poorly. There are many processed foods around and lots of standard junk food is accidentally Vegan. A diet of french fries, skittles, onion rings, and toast, will make anyone ill, so it's important to note that people of all diets can be eating poorly and can become ill because of it. But if you eat a normal, whole foods, plant based diet, you will see many benefits to your health. Governments and health authorities are endorsing plant based vegan diets for all ages now; it is no longer a strange lifestyle choice and it shouldn't be treated as one anymore.

Compare a normal varied Vegan diet with a normal Western Diet and you will find the Vegans come out on top as far as health and longevity go. Diseases and illnesses, as mentioned earlier, are the biggest killers of humans around the world. To ignore this and instead focus on the few Vegans that become ill because they haven't eaten properly is disingenuous to say the least.

How many people die from Heart Disease, high blood pressure, cancer, and diabetes each year compared to Vegans with a poor diet? I'm pretty sure the difference will be gargantuan. Spend an hour looking at studies and research reports, and you will clearly see meat is responsible for so much disease and death. We came across a book by Dr Michael Greger that is packed with research from very credible sources. It has pages and pages of links to resources so you can go and read for yourself. We wrote a blog about this on our website if you would like to find out more. The details are also in the Bibliography of this book.

Insinuating that the Vegan diet is bad for our health is like saying breathing is killing us. We want to grow old and give ourselves the greatest chance of a long and healthy life as possible. Sure, we can become ill due to genetics but why increase the odds? A Vegan diet, properly researched and explored, will give us the best chance of not just growing old, but growing old and remaining in good health. We are all guilty of focussing on the here and now and looking for instant gratification and pleasure, especially from our food. However, good choices can be made for the short term whilst also benefiting our future selves. I want to grow old and be active and full of energy, and I imagine a time when I will look back and thank my self for making the decision to look after my body and Go Vegan!

CHAPTER 24

WHERE DO YOU GET CALCIUM?

"One farmer says to me, 'You cannot live on vegetable food solely, for it furnishes nothing to make the bones with;' and so he religiously devotes a part of his day to supplying himself with the raw material of bones; walking all the while he talks behind his oxen, which, with vegetable-made bones, jerk him and his lumbering plow along in spite of every obstacle."

- Henry David Thereau

Like most things, Calcium just isn't a problem for vegans. The dairy industry has done a great job of making everyone believe that cows milk is the only source of calcium. It just isn't true. You can find calcium in high quantities in dark leafy greens especially Kale, spinach, broccoli, cabbage, and okra.

The great thing about a vegan diet, is that you are more aware of what you are eating and the benefits you get from the foods. This awareness leads to a healthy lifestyle with far less dietary deficiencies than a typical western meat eating diet.

Casein in milk and animal proteins has even been suggested to actually hinder the absorption process of calcium, so although milk is high in calcium, the absorption is low. Milk is also fortified with calcium now, so you are really consuming a supplement rather than the calcium that is found naturally in the milk.

If you don't think you can get enough calcium through eating green vegetables - even though you certainly can - then you can support your diet with lots of vegan friendly foods that have calcium added to them. Things like soya milk, tofu, and cereals are all often fortified with calcium.

Calcium deficiency in vegans is just another misconception and once we have the facts revealed to us, we know that we just don't need animal products to get the nutrients, minerals, and vitamins we need.

CHAPTER 25

WHERE DO YOU GET PROTEIN?

"I do feel that spiritual progress does demand at some stage that we should cease to kill our fellow creatures for the satisfaction of our bodily wants."

- Mohanda Ghandi

If you are a vegan or are considering the move to a plant based diet, you will undoubtedly have people ask you, "where will you get your protein?" I can predict you will hear this question from almost every new person you speak to about your vegan diet. Because this is such a popular question, I decided to go a little deeper and devote a whole chapter to it.

Protein is essential for our bodies, but it doesn't only come from meat, eggs, fish and dairy. Most foods contain protein, some in large amounts, others in small amounts. Nuts, seeds, legumes, beans and lentils are all high in protein. Even broccoli contains a considerable amount of protein and since becoming a vegan, it's my favourite vegetable. I have written a blog post about broccoli on our website. Have a read, it's amazing what one vegetable can do for you!

Protein is very important for us, but no more necessary than fats and carbohydrates (macro nutrients), or vitamins and minerals (micro nutrients).

So what exactly is Protein? Simply put, protein is a type of molecule made up of chains of amino acids. These protein molecules make up the structural parts of our body, amongst other things. Your organs, immune system, muscles, and other bodily tissues, are mostly made up of protein. You need to consume protein in order to maintain, replace and repair them. Specific protein molecules are also used to make the haemoglobin in the red blood cells that carry oxygen around your body. Other proteins build your heart muscle, your bones, protect you from disease, and work in the muscles to move your body.

How does it do all this? I am no biologist, but I can give a terse description of the process. The process begins when we eat foods that contain protein. Our stomach and intestines digest the protein and break it down into smaller molecules called amino acids (hydrolysis). These amino acids are then sent through the blood stream and are reassembled to build the specific proteins that our body needs (condensation).

There are many different amino acids and the different combinations make up different proteins. Twenty two of these amino acids are the most important for us. Our body can make thirteen of them naturally, but the other nine have to be acquired by eating proteins in foods and then digesting to break them up. These nine are called 'essential amino acids'. We have to get these for our body to function correctly, so it is important that we make sure we eat foods that contain them all.

You will hear a lot about 'complete proteins.' There is a fallacy that there are better quality proteins than others. This is due, in the most part, to the meat and dairy industry and years of marketing and propaganda. It's true that meat, eggs, fish, and dairy contain what are known as 'complete proteins'; they contain all of the nine essential amino acids. This doesn't make them better in any way though, as we can get all the essential amino acids from a variety of plant based sources.

In order to get all the essential amino acids from plant based sources we simply have to eat a variety of them. It is important that the variety are eaten together in combinations, or you can even eat them individually throughout the day. You can have rice and black beans together, for example. This simple combination gives you all your essential amino acids. So a chilli con carne is perfect. You could also have wholegrain bread with peanut butter.

There are other advantages to getting all your protein from plant based foods. You get more fibre, less bad fats, more vitamins and minerals, and, most importantly, nothing has to be needlessly killed for you to eat.

How much protein do we need? On average, adults need about 60-100 grams per day. There are some studies that suggest plant based proteins are not as easily digested, so you could aim for the higher 100 grams per day if you want. You can also work it out on your own body weight by allowing 0.6-0.8 grams of protein per kilo of body weight.

For children it's a bit different. A good way to calculate is to allow 1 gram or protein per kilo of body weight, slightly more per kilo than an adult, but less total grams overall.

So where can vegans get protein? Most foods have protein. Nuts, fruits, vegetables, they all have it. As a good rule of thumb, as long as you eat a varied diet and meet your calorie needs, you will get enough protein. Plant based sources of protein are plentiful. Nuts and seeds are very high in protein, as well as oats, tofu and beans.

Most people don't know much about protein, I know I didn't before I was a vegan. They don't know what it is, how much you need, and where you can get it. I put this down to decades of brainwashing by the meat and dairy industries, convincing us that we can only get protein from their dead animal produce.

There are a couple of ways to approach this. You can just ask them exactly how much protein you need. If they know the answer to this then there is a good chance that they know where you can get it from and then probably wouldn't have asked you in the first place!

Asking them this will highlight to them that they don't really know what they are talking about. Go further if you need to, ask them what protein is too.

Probably the best and non-snarky way is to say something a bit like this:

"I used to think that to. But then I researched exactly what protein is, how much I need, and where I can get it. We only need 0.6-0.8 grams of protein per kilo of body weight per day. I can easily get all this from fruits, nuts, and vegetables, as long as I eat 2000-2500 calories. Eating a varied diet makes sure I get all the essential amino acids that my body needs to make all the different proteins. The best part is that my protein comes without saturated fats and cholesterol, and is packed with fibre to help me digest and breakdown my food. Protein really isn't an issue for vegans."

You could offer to point them to a resource to learn more about protein just to seal the deal.

If this is still not enough, then you can point out some famous sports athletes who are vegan. 300lb NFL player, David Carter, is a vegan. Ultra Marathon Runner, Scott Jurek. UFC Fighter, Nick Diaz. Olympic Gold Medal Rower, David Smith. Pro Surfer and World Champion, Tia Blanco. 8 time national super heavyweight boxing champion, Cam Awesome. World leading climber, Steph Davis. Germany's strongest man and power lifter, Patrik Baboumian. American weightlifting record holder, Kendrick Farris. All Vegan.

All these professional world record holding athletes get all the protein they need from a vegan plant based diet. Imagine how much money and time they have invested to find a perfect diet so they can push their bodies to achieve maximum results? They would not be on a vegan plant based diet if it wasn't healthy. It is the optimum choice for them.

Even after all this, when we first started our plant based diet we were concerned that we might not get enough protein, and thought it would be good to monitor our protein intake. We had been misguided for so many years and it was difficult to disregard everything we had been told overnight. To help us, we used a free website called www.cronometer.com

This site lets you enter everything you eat into a database that breaks down all your macro and micro nutrients. It gives you a full count of everything you are eating, and points out gaps that you need to fill in order to hit the recommended targets of all the carbohydrates, lipids, proteins, vitamins and minerals.

After only a week, we were so confident that we were getting everything we needed from our new plant based vegan diet that we only used it every few days and now we don't use it often at all. It's so easy to get all your protein each day just from eating a variety of foods and as long as you do have a variety, you just don't have to worry as you will naturally hit the targets without even trying.

www.cronometer.com is a great tool and if you give it a go you will see that there are some macro and micro nutrients that are hard to get from plant based sources. Vitamins B12 and D, and Omega fatty acids. Don't worry though, these can be found in fortified foods and taken as supplements. You can also target specific foods such as nuts and seeds to make sure you get enough.

Protein is the question I think you will encounter the most, so I hope this chapter gives you all the information you need to address the protein argument. Once you address it, the usual response is to throw another objection at you. But this is good! The more questions they ask or the more objections they give you, the more opportunities you will have to promote the vegan message and move them one step closer to being a vegan themselves.

CHAPTER 26

YOU CAN'T GET B12 IN A VEGAN DIET

"Take care of your body, it's the only place you have to live."

- Jim Rohn

In our modern sterilised world, Vegans are more likely to become vitamin B12 deficient than anyone else, so finding sources of vitamin B12 for Vegans is important. While it can take some time to become deficient in vitamin B12, it doesn't mean you should avoid taking measures early on.

You will no doubt hear concerns from family and friends when you talk about your new plant-based diet. But you don't have to worry about B12 as long as you are aware of what it is, why you need it, how much you need, and where you can get it from. Just eat foods fortified with B12 and take a supplement, and you will have nothing to worry about.

Since my family and I chose our plant-based diet, we have been taking Vitamin B complex supplements. Our children take a multi-vitamin each day from 'Well Kids'. Both are suitable for vegans and don't cost much at all. Our vitamin B complex cost very little, and I don't even take one a day. I take one every 2 or 3 days, as many foods I eat are already fortified with B12. There are many options available, so shop around to find the right one for you and your family. The Well Kids multivitamins are our favourite, between £4–£7.50 for 30 tablets. They are packed with many important vitamins and minerals. For just over £5 a month, we are buying the peace of mind that are children are getting all the vitamins they need and any nutritional gaps we miss with our menus are filled.

It seems Vegans are not the only ones at risk though. A study called The Framingham Offspring Study, found that 39% of the general population may be low and deficient in B12. Obviously this included all diets, vegan, vegetarian and omnivore. It was interesting to read that the percentage of the population that had the highest 'normal' B12 levels, were those that that took B12 supplements or ate food that was supplemented with B12.

Meat eaters can get some B12 from the meat, dairy, and eggs they eat. However, it's interesting to note that animals are given B12 supplements either in their feed or by injections. So whether you eat meat or not, your B12 is coming from a supplement of some kind.

B12 is naturally found in untreated water, untreated soil and in the bacteria in our stomachs. Once we started to treat water and use chemicals in our soils, levels of B12 are greatly reduced. Cattle in factory farms are no longer eating the fresh grass in B12 rich fields that have been fertilised with their own faeces that has been trampled into the earth. This is why they are no longer getting enough B12 and need injections or supplements in their own food. The antibiotics kill the B12 producing bacteria in their guts and then they need to be supplemented. Pesticides also kill the B12 producing bacteria on our fruits and vegetables. Now we no longer drink from a stream, eat vegetables grown in B12 rich soil, have replaced leaves for toilet paper, and make sure we wash our hands, we just aren't getting the B12 we need in our diet.

Vitamin B12 is a nutrient that helps keep the body's nerve and blood cells healthy. It helps make DNA, the genetic material in all cells. Vitamin B12 also helps prevent a type of anemia called megaloblastic anemia that makes people tired and weak. Two steps are required for the body to absorb vitamin B12 from food. First, hydrochloric acid in the stomach separates vitamin B12 from the protein to which vitamin B12 is attached in food. After this, vitamin B12 combines with a protein made by the stomach called intrinsic factor and is absorbed by the body. Some people have pernicious anemia, a condition where they cannot make intrinsic factor. As a result, they have trouble absorbing vitamin B12 from all foods and dietary supplements.

How much do we need? The amount of vitamin B12 you need each day depends on your age. Average daily recommended amounts for different ages are listed below in micrograms (mcg):

Life Stage	Recommended Amount
Birth to 6 months	0.4 mcg
Infants 7–12 months	0.5 mcg
Children 1–3 years	0.9 mcg
Children 4–8 years	1.2 mcg

Children 9–13 years	1.8 mcg
Teens 14–18 years	2.4 mcg
Adults	2.4 mcg
Pregnant teens and women	2.6 mcg
Breastfeeding teens and women	2.8 mcg

It's true that vitamin B12 is not present in fruits, nuts, and vegetables. So for this reason Vegans have to take supplements or eat foods that have been fortified with vegan B12 produced from bacteria like yeast.

Lots of foods like cereals, dairy alternatives, and spreads, are fortified with vitamin B12. You can also get it from yeast products. There are some other products that contain B12, such as spirulina. But be warned, these may not be able to give you enough B12. Here is an excerpt from the Vegan Society:

'Claimed sources of B12 that have been shown through direct studies of vegans to be inadequate include human gut bacteria, spirulina, dried nori, barley grass and most other seaweeds. Several studies of raw food vegans have shown that raw food offers no special protection.'

When we had a pet rabbit, we noticed she used to eat her own poo. At first we thought this was gross, so we checked in a rabbit book to see if this was normal. It turns out that rabbits, guinea pigs, and other animals have to eat their poo to get the B12 from it. Because B12 is created by our own bodily bacteria in the gut, we can't absorb it and it is excreted in our faeces. So in theory, we could get B12 from eating our own poo, but getting volunteers to test the theory might be tricky!

There are some great sources of Vitamin B12 for Vegans. Nutritional Yeast is great to add to sauces, stews, soups and pretty much any savoury dishes. It gives a cheesy, nutty flavour. When we first bought it, we were a bit unsure of the appearance. It looks just like fish food! But now we are used to it, we add it to a lot of our meals.

Love it or hate it, Marmite is a great source of Vitamin B12! We love Marmite and eat tons of the stuff on toast, crackers and in sandwiches. You can even add it to a source or a favourite of mine is to pop in with roast potatoes to give a real unique savoury flavour.

Lots of dairy alternatives are fortified with B12. Check the labels, though, just to be sure.

Some people might object to supplements, saying it's not natural. You may get this response that it can't be natural to be a vegan because we need B12 and you can't find B12 in non meat products. To argue this, just go back to the water and soil information. Our modern world had removed us from the natural way of things and has removed the natural B12 we would get from drinking from streams and natural water sources and eating fruits and vegetables with B12 rich soil.

Just what is natural anymore anyway? Is it natural that the B12 we would have been able to get naturally is not available because of all the unnatural farming and agriculture methods us humans have developed and adopted? It's not natural to do most of the things we do and eat most of the things we eat, but we do them anyway. I will happily take an unnatural supplement if it means we don't have to unnaturally kill billions of animals every year to receive the B12 they have been given unnaturally in the first place.

CHAPTER 27

WHAT ABOUT VITAMIN D?

"A single sunbeam is enough to drive away many shadows."

- St Francis of Assisi

Vitamin D is created by our bodies using a process involving direct sunlight and helps with the absorption of calcium. Without it, our bones can become weak and we can experience pains in our bones and tenderness in our joints.

Going out in the sun for 30 minutes each day with your forearms and head exposed, should be enough to ensure your body can create enough vitamin D for your needs. In the UK, the NHS recommends that you can get enough Vitamin D to last all year just by exposing your skin to the sun between March and September. The time varies for everyone and depends on skin colour and other issues. You can obviously spend too long in the sun, so be careful not to burn. There are lots of guidelines, especially for children and during pregnancy, so you might want to have a look at the NHS website.

If you don't go out much or like to keep covered up, then a supplement would be a good idea. Many foods are fortified with vitamin D, especially cereals and dairy alternatives, so the chances are you are already taking a supplement of some kind without realising it.

Being a Vegan doesn't mean you can't get your vitamin D needs met. Going out in the sun, eating fortified foods, and supplementing is all you need to do, and after a few weeks, you will know how much vitamin D you are consuming on a typical day so you won't have to keep measuring it. Meat eaters still need to get out in the sun too, and shouldn't rely on meat and dairy for their hit of D. Sitting behind a keyboard, trolling vegans, and eating KFC and bacon sandwiches just wont cut it!

CHAPTER 28

WHAT ABOUT IRON?

"Everything has it's limit - Iron ore cannot be educated into Gold."

- Mark Twain

As with most nutrients, vitamins, and minerals, Iron can be consumed in sufficient quantities so long as you eat a varied and balanced diet. Vitamin C can help the absorption of Iron so it's a good idea to combine the two during a meal if possible.

Combining leafy greens with other foods that are high in vitamin C will increase the absorption levels. Broccoli is really good as it is high in both calcium and vitamin C. Other options could be a nice green salad with a lime dressing or have a glass of fruit juice or a smoothy with your leafy green rich meal.

If you want to be cautious, then you can take a multi-vitamin or Iron supplement and also eat foods that are fortified with iron.

As with the Protein objection, you could ask your meat eating friend what Iron is, what it does, how much we need and where we can get it. If they have the answers then they shouldn't be asking the question.

CHAPTER 29

CAN'T DIGEST CELLULOSE

"Every noble life leaves it's fibre interwoven forever in the work of the world."

- John Ruskin

A recent argument I've heard is that humans can't digest cellulose. But what is it? Cellulose is the structural component of fruits, grains, and vegetables. Cells in animals don't have cell walls but fruits, grains, and vegetables do. These cell walls are the structural element known as cellulose. Vegans only eat fruits, plants, and vegetables, so how on earth are any vegans still alive if they cannot digest the only food they eat?

Simply put, cellulose is dietary fibre. It goes through our digestive system just like any other food, but the actual fibre molecules remain intact and aren't digested by the enzymes in our small intestines. As a carbohydrate, fibre is formed of sugars, but because these sugars are not digested, they don't get absorbed by our body. Fibre molecules are degraded by bacteria during a fermentation process in our colon which explains why high fibre diets can cause gas and bloating.

We need dietary fibre because it has important effects on nutrients in the small intestine. It also helps the large intestine and has lots of important health benefits. It helps digestion and the absorption of fats and glucose in the small intestine. It also fuels the bacteria in our large intestine, which help us to make vitamin B12. Fatty acids are released from the dietary fibre which are essential for a healthy colon. Fibre speeds up the removal of toxins and waste from our body whilst keeping us regular, which is important in reducing the risk of cancers.

You can have too much dietary fibre, however, so there are a few things to keep in mind to make sure you don't have too much in your diet. Too much can give you stomach cramps and wind. It can impair the absorption of minerals such as zinc, iron, and calcium. This is why it's very important to drink plenty of water and keep hydrated. In the UK, the NHS recommends 30 grams of fibre per day, but on average, most people on a standard meat eating diet only get 18 grams.

So it's very evident that we need fibre in our diet for a healthy gut, and there are many benefits. On average, meat eaters are fibre deficient, but have no idea about this. I know I didn't before I was a vegan. Vegans can often find ourselves under the scrutiny of people who have no idea what they are talking about. I think that they don't mean any harm when they scrutinise our diet and worry about our deficiencies. I just think they have been the victims of centuries of manipulation and marketing to believe their diet is perfect and healthy for them and ours isn't.

SECTION 4 - ENVIRONMENT

CHAPTER 30

VEGANS KILL MORE ANIMALS

"Do we have the right to rear animals in order to kill them so that we may feed appetites in which we have been artificially conditioned from childhood?"

- Ashley Montagu

Around 70 Billion land animals and 90 billion marine animals are intentionally killed every year. These land animals are fed 40% of the worlds grain crops just to fatten them up for us to eat.

Animals such as snakes, mice, and insects, are killed by the machinery used in farming, no doubt about it, but these wild creatures are not killed intentionally. They are not artificially bred by us, imprisoned by us, and killed by is in the billions. Their death is accidental rather than booked in with a slaughter house. Their death is not a scheduled execution that is known from the day they are born.

If we stopped eating meat, then the amount of grain grown would be greatly reduced and, therefore, the amount of animals accidentally killed during the harvest process would be greatly reduced too. So eating meat is responsible for both accidental and intentional harm and death to the animals. Eating a plant based diet would only be responsible for a reduced amount of accidental harm and death. It's all about intention.

We could even improve on the methods used to harvest crops. A fraction of the money given to meat farmers in the form of government subsidies, could be put to good use to come up new ideas and methods that stopped animals being harmed in the process of crop farming. If we all started to think vegan then we could stop the intentional cruelty and death and greatly reduce the accidental too. We want to minimise harm, not promote more death.

But could it be argued that the intent to farm, when you know deaths will occur, is an intent to harm which would make the accidental deaths actually intentional? A good point perhaps, and I have thought about this for some time. Compare it to swimming. We know that people drown when they go swimming. Going swimming always brings with it a very small risk of drowning. So if we take a child swimming, and they drown, is it our fault? People die falling out of bed too, so are we guilty of causing intentional harm by tucking our children into bed each night?

If we don't farm, we die. If we don't learn to swim, we could drown. If we don't sleep, we die. We have to eat, learn to swim, and sleep to prolong our lives and to exist on this planet at all. So you could argue that everything we do has consequences, and if we know these consequences we are guilty of committing harm to everyone and everything around us every minute of every day.

If we want to live then some animals will be harmed and will die, but, and this is a big but, we are not choosing to kill them to eat them when we don't have to. When someone chooses to kill and eat animals when they know they don't have to, that truly is intent to cause necessary harm and cannot in any way be compared with the accidental harm and death caused by our very existence in the world.

Now if someone knows the facts about the unnecessary animal suffering, unnecessary cruelty, and unnecessary death, will they choose to continue to cause harm or will they stop it? If they carry on, what kind of person does that make them?

CHAPTER 31

WITHOUT MANURE WE WOULDN'T BE ABLE TO GROW ANY FOOD CROPS

"The civilisation of one epoch becomes the manure of the next."

- Cyril Connolly

Some people think that we need animal manure to grow all the vegetables. But what exactly is manure? Manure is defined as:

"Manure is organic matter, mostly derived from animal faeces except in the case of green manure, which can be used as organic fertilizer in agriculture. Manures contribute to the fertility of the soil by adding organic matter and nutrients, such as nitrogen, that are trapped by bacteria in the soil."

So although when we think of manure we imagine animal droppings, manure can also be produced from rotting plants.

Fritz Haber was a German chemist who you may have heard of. In 1918, he created a process called 'Haber-Bosch', which is the method used in industry in the synthesis of fertilisers and explosives on a massive scale. In fact, half the worlds population would not be sustained without this method being used to produce nitrogen fertilisers. As with many German scientists around that time, Haber's inventions were also put to use in warfare resulting in many deaths. So, sadly, his Nobel Prize winning invention was responsible for taking and also sustaining many lives.

So with this process and the green plant based manure, animal waste is just not necessary. Fish are also used in the fertilisation of soil in certain parts of the world, and the oceans are suffering because of it. This could be eliminated too. With so many crops being grown to feed the 70 billion land animals we kill every year, not eating meat would mean we would reduce the amount of fertiliser we need to feed the world. Also, we can stop taking all the plant based resources away from the poorer countries to feed the cattle being raised in the more developed ones.

Even if we did need animals to graze and add manure to fields for growing crops, that doesn't automatically mean we have to eat them! All around, a green manure fertiliser is achievable and the best option for the planet. Adopting greener farming methods will reduce the chemicals we have to treat crops with, and the removal of animal food products will result in so many other benefits for our health, the environment, and especially the poor animals.

CHAPTER 32

WHAT WOULD THE COUNTRYSIDE LOOK LIKE WITHOUT ANIMALS?

"Come forth into the light of things, let nature be your teacher."

- William Wordsworth

This is a strange one and when we were asked it, we didn't really have an answer prepared. Often, people will not really think about the alternatives and when they are not aware of the suffering and abuse animals suffer, questions like this would seem quite legitimate to them. To us Vegans, it's awful!

Putting 'a nice countryside view' over the lives of animals is quite odd. It implies that we are the centre of the universe and everything around us has to be tailored to match our idea of how our surroundings should be. The English countryside should be fields with neat walls and hedges, fencing in live stock of some kind. Imagine if this aesthetic carried on to the slaughter process and the abattoirs didn't have any walls? Would the view be so appealing I wonder?

So to address this objection, we have to ask if the person is aware of just exactly what the animals go through during their time in and around the fields and farming process. We can refer to the section on 'Factory Farming Doesn't Hurt Animals' to highlight the terrible conditions they face or the awful process they go through in having their tails docked and other gruesome acts. We should also talk about the dairy industry and the horrendous cycle the cows face to produce milk and dairy products.

If, after knowing all this, they are still sure they would rather have the nice view and a glass of milk, then perhaps the conversation won't go in the direction you would like. If the person can't make the connection with their nice view and the suffering the animals endure, then it is very sad indeed. I would rather see a country that had no animals on display especially animals that were being imprisoned, raped, murdered, and eaten. Let the fields grow with colourful crops instead or allow forests to reclaim places where they once stood.

When I started to write this book, we were living in a Cornish village and all around us were beautiful fields. We took our dog out each day and walked past a couple of small fields with sheep in. We would even hear them bleating each evening around feeding time. It was nice to see them and notice all their different faces, but sometimes we would go by the field and for weeks they would be empty. We were not sad because we couldn't see them anymore. We were sad because we knew they had been sent to slaughter and had been eaten not long after.

So what do I think the countryside would look like if no one ate animals? Peaceful.

CHAPTER 33

FARMING DOESN'T IMPACT THE ENVIRONMENT

"The greatest threat to our planet is the belief that someone else will save it."

- Robert Swan

Anyone who says that farming doesn't impact the environment must not live on the same planet as us! You only have to look around to see fields, fences, stone walls, tracks, and plenty of other evidence to show that farming has completely changed our landscape. And this is just what we can see on a daily basis around our homes and towns.

All around the world, factory farms are causing nitrous oxide gas on a massive scale. Animal waste pollutes streams and rivers and deforestation is destroying the rainforests to make way for more cattle and more cattle feed. Rainforests are being designated to grow palm sugar and mono-agriculture is ruining the top soil.

There is no denying any of this, yet people still do. In order to kill 150 billion sentient beings every year, the environment has had to suffer. Just imagine how much space is needed to house these animals and grow their food. How many lorries and facilities are needed to transport the live animals, kill them, and package their flesh as meat products that we see on the supermarket shelves.

And what about fish farms? These are responsible for the destruction of our ocean habitats and it has been forecast that the oceans could be empty of fish by 2050 if we carry on as we are doing. With human population growing and the demand for meat and fish growing with it, something has to change and fast.

Pretending that farming has no impact on our planet just so you can carry on eating meat, eggs, dairy, and fish, is totally irresponsible, not just to yourself, but to the future generations.

CHAPTER 34

IF WE DON'T EAT ANIMALS WE WOULD HAVE TO GROW MORE CROPS WHICH WOULD CAUSE MORE DESTRUCTION

"Animals are my friends . . . And I don't eat my friends."

- George Bernard Shaw

The idea that if we didn't eat animals we would have to grow more crops, might seem like a genuine objection on the meat eaters part, but it doesn't take long to unpack it and point out that it just isn't true.

With over 150 billion sentient beings killed every year, and only 7 billion humans on the planet, does it seem logical that we would eat more crops than all these animals do right now? What if we only had to grow crops to feed 7 billion humans and no animals? Would we grow less crops or more?

I think these are reasonable questions to ask. It seems obvious to me that we wouldn't grow more crops. Yes, many of the 150 billion are small chickens and fish, but billions are also big pigs and cows, and they need a lot of calories to sustain their bulk.

The animals we eat have been eating something for months even years before we eat them and their products, like dairy and eggs. What have they been eating? The Council for Agricultural Science and Technology (CAST) 1999 Animal Agriculture and Global Food Supply Report states that an average of 8 pounds of grain is used to produce a pound of beef. It takes about 2 pounds of grain to produce 1 pound of chicken and about 4 pounds of grain to produce 1 pound of pork. Then add on all the fuel, land, water, and other resources required to grow, harvest, store, and transport the additional crops plus the resources to keep, transport, and slaughter the animals.

It's not just crops that we grow to feed them though. The oceans are being drained of fish to mash up into feed for animals. This is not a common thing we are told about, but the oceans off of Peru are being pillaged on an industrial scale and the fish populations are not being given time to recover. We need the oceans to survive on this planet so not draining them of all life just to feed to animals we will also kill then eat, would be a very good thing to do.

So if the animals were not bred then the level of crops grown would certainly not be an issue and after a few years the oceans would start to be healthy and full of life again. There would also be other benefits. More land would be available, the rainforests wouldn't have to be destroyed on such scale, less pollution from the reservoirs of animal waste that are a result of factory farming, and no more government subsidies going to foods that are harmful to us, our morality, the animals, and the planet. We could use the tax payers money that would be saved to improve healthcare, education, science, and many, many other areas. There would be less people affected by obesity, heart disease, diabetes, and basically all the top killers of human beings. World hunger could be solved. The negatives? A handful of people would not be as wealthy.

CHAPTER 35

PEOPLE IN EXTREME ENVIRONMENTS NEED TO EAT MEAT

"It is not the strongest of the species that survives, nor the most intelligent that survives. It is the one that is most adaptable to change."

- Charles Darwin

There are groups of people and tribes around the world that just have to eat meat, or drink milk, to survive. In Africa, there is a tribe that drink the milk and blood of their cattle. They live in a hostile environment where crops are difficult to grow and they are so far away from society that purchasing fresh produce regularly is impossible. In the Amazon, tribes still live off the land there. They track and hunt animals to eat and really do make use of every part of who they kill. For these types of people, meat and milk is an important part of their diet and without it they would probably not live long or well.

Here's the important thing to consider though, most of us don't live in the African waste land or the Amazon rainforest. We live in a society that has a shop on every corner filled with more food than we will ever need. These shops have non-animal alternatives that give us every nutrient, vitamin, mineral, protein, carbohydrate, and fat that our body needs to be healthy and thrive.

Another point is that the people in Africa or the Amazon do not trash their environment. They only take what they need and they don't overpopulate to the point where they use up and destroy all the resources available to them. Hunters don't always catch an animal, and often they will only eat meat once or twice a week and they certainly don't imprison and breed animals to fuel their hunger. They are co-dependent on their environment and are part of the ecosystem rather than separate from it.

If I lived in a tribe like these then obviously I would be eating meat too, but I don't! I don't and neither do most of the world's population. The meat that most of the world eats isn't hunted or living with them and moving with them around the desert following sources of water. Their meat comes from a horrendous source that we vegans are all too aware of. It's packaged, wrapped, shaped, formed, and flavoured and is so far from being an animal that most people couldn't tell you which animals flesh they were eating if it wasn't labelled or printed on a menu.

These arguments detract from the suffering encountered by the animals eaten by most people. The reality is we don't live in extreme conditions and we can't use that as a reason to eat animals. We have an abundance of delicious healthy food available all year round for us to enjoy and thrive on.

CHAPTER 36

BACON VS LETTUCE

"Wisdom begins in wonder."

- Socrates

Eating lettuce is bad for the planet. We need to eat bacon if we really want to save the world!

In 2015, a study was conducted that looked at the water footprint and greenhouse gas emissions per calorie for a variety of foods. The media chose to take two very different foods and highlight the difference between them in a clickbait style rouse to elicit readers, likes, and shares. They reported how a single calorie of lettuce creates more greenhouse gases than a single calorie of bacon. So should we all be eating bacon if we want to save the planet?

Fortunately there are a few things we can bring to the attention of the click bait victims. First, let's think about what it means to compare bacon to lettuce on a calorific level. Bacon has approxiamatley 500-550 calories per 100 grams. If we wanted to eat 500-550 calories of lettuce, we would need to eat 6-6.5 whole lettuce! Chopping that lettuce to make a sandwich would increase the volume of lettuce to such a size that a lettuce sandwich would be over 3 feet (90cm) tall!

Second, the click baiters left out all of the other foods that were mentioned in the study. Lots of food items produce much lower amounts of greenhouse gas emissions than bacon and other meat products. Spinach, wheat, potatoes, rice, kale, and broccoli, all came in as much better options. Now if we compare all of those calorifically against bacon, the vegetables will come out as winners in all areas. Meat consumption was shown to be the highest producer of greenhouse gases when looked at as a group. Vegetables, as a group, were then obviously found to be producing less.

Examples of manipulated studies by the media just to gain readership, do not help anyone except the shareholders. Luckily, the internet makes it easy for almost anyone to access the actual studies and read the facts for themselves. We are no longer in a position where we have to rely on the media and their lies to miseducate us anymore.

CHAPTER 37

VEGANS KILL PLANTS

"I must have flowers, always and always."

- Claude Monet

This one will come up a lot. Some might be serious but most people think it's funny and when I hear it, I know they don't take the killing of animals seriously. However, rather than ignore it, I feel it is my duty to give it a sensible reply. You never know, some words may get through their protective meat jacket and have a snowball effect, rolling them further along towards their vegan snowman!

I can't put myself in the persons shoes with this objection, so I usually just start with a question: 'Do you really think a carrot is the same as a pig? Is cutting up a carrot the same as cutting up a pig?'

The response should be, 'of course not,' but I quickly realised this won't always be the case. Meat eaters like to eat meat and many will cling to any excuse they can think of to give themselves a guilt free pass to do so. So you may have to go further.

Plants and animals are different in so many ways. Tear off a part of a plant, repot it, or place it the ground and with a little water, sunshine, and time that part will grow into a plant of it's own. Now imagine doing the same with a human. Tear of a finger, or even an arm. Pop that in the ground next to your plant part. Water it, give it sunshine, and some time. We all know what happens.

Plants are not sentient beings. Animals are. There is no research or evidence to show otherwise. Carrots do not have brains, nervous systems or organs. They are not sentient beings.

If the person is so concerned about the death of vegetables, then point out that more vegetables are consumed by the billions of animals that are killed each year than by people. If they didn't eat animals then they wouldn't be responsible for killing as many vegetables. So Vegans are responsible for 'killing' far fewer vegetables than meat eaters. What's worse, meat eaters eat the animals that have eaten lot's of vegetables and they eat vegetables too! Vegans are not killing any sentient beings and are (if it was possible to) killing far less vegetables too.

Even if we all agreed it is wrong to eat non-sentient vegetables, then that doesn't mean we should escalate our wrongness and eat sentient animals too. That's like saying, well I found a ten pound note on the floor and picked it up, so now I should go and rob a bank.

Although we are obligated to keep our production of plants to a sustainable level, ensuring we do not damage the planet while doing so, there is no reason why we should treat them as we treat sentient loving animals.

CHAPTER 38

VEGANS EAT ANIMALS FOOD

"You have just dined, and however scrupulously the slaughterhouse is concealed in the graceful distance of miles, there is complicity."

- Ralph Waldo Emerson

I would rather eat the same food as an animal, than eat the animal itself. Just because the food we eat is similar, doesn't mean the animals suffer or go hungry because we eat it.

Vegans just don't eat the animals food though. They may eat similar food, but in no way do vegans take food away from animals making them starve. In fact, most soya and other crops grown for animal feed, are actually taking food away from humans! Crops are grown in poorer countries, devastating the environments in the process, before being shipped to richer countries to feed up the animals that the richer humans will eventually eat.

As long as humans still have the desire to eat the flesh of animals the animals will have no shortage of food. Eating animal flesh not only hurts the animals needlessly, but it also takes food away from humans and is a serious contributor to world hunger.

CHAPTER 39

YOU CARE MORE ABOUT ANIMALS THAN HUMANS

"It takes nothing away from a human to be kind to an animal."

- Joaquin Phoenix

Why do you people say this? It is as if we can't care about more than one thing at the same time. Veganism could actually be one way to stop the human suffering too. If we didn't have to grow so much food for the animals that get eaten, then we could grow that food for the people who are starving around the world.

I can care for both animals and humans and one thing I can do right away is choose to stop eating them. I can literally help the animals by changing my diet and being responsible about what I eat. How many things are there in the world that are disgusting or outrageous that we wish we could change but have no power to? With the animal issue, we can actually make a difference immediately. The more people that go Vegan, the more animals are prevented from being bred, tortured, confined, and killed. It's as simple as that.

Everything is linked. Animals being bred on huge scales affect areas that people live in. By protecting one we are protecting the other; they work hand in hand. Ignoring the suffering of animals in factory farming is giving silent permission for the atrocities to affect the people that are tied up in the process too. Anyone who really cares about other people around the world, the amazon or Africa for example, would look at what their lifestyle causes and then start to make changes. One immediate change that benefits everyone is to go Vegan. You can make that decision and that same day make a difference. How can anyone not make that decision?

Water sources across the world are being bought up and controlled. Aquifers are being drained to keep industries going. Corporations are removing people from their land and as we have seen in South America, people are being killed for standing up against their activities.

Animals suffer just as we do. They feel pain, they grieve, and they experience emotions the same as us. Over 150 billion sentient are being killed each year. More animals are killed in one year than the total number of humans that have ever existed! Whole species are being made extinct in huge numbers every day as we bulldoze through their environments and torch their habitat. This is mass murder on an unimaginable scale. Just try counting to 150 billion to represent each animal. It would take you over 4,950 years if you could count one number every second without stopping. These numbers are so big that we just can't fathom them.

With such atrocities happening all around us, how can we not choose to protect these animals and stop this unecesary bloodshed? What sort of person would I be if just looked the other way, or worse, joined in? The sad truth is, I would be normal.

CHAPTER 40

WHAT ABOUR WARS AND FAMINE?

"As long as man continues to be the ruthless destroyer of lower living beings he will never know health or peace. For as long as men massacre animals, they will kill each other. Indeed, he who sows the seed of murder and pain cannot reap joy and love."

- Pythagoras

This is really just like the Caring About Humans More Section. Standing up for one atrocity does not rule out the capability of an individual to stand up for other issues. I often wonder why a person would make this comment. I also wonder if they are actually doing anything to stand up against the wars, famine, and other areas they seem so concerned with.

Choosing to go vegan has a knock on effect on all areas. Not eating animals would mean we could grow more crops to feed to humans that are starving. If the whole world was not consuming dead flesh, perhaps our blood lust would not be such a dominant feature of our humanity? Not eating animals and farming them on huge scales would mean we wouldn't need to fight over land or resources anymore.

This is why I think Veganism really is the answer for everything, or, at the very least, our first step in making the world a safer and more peaceful place. Choosing to go vegan will allow humanity to take giant leaps forward in our morality, our health, and the health of the planet.

CHAPTER 41

THE ECONOMY WOULD CRASH

"Economy does not lie in sparing money, but in spending it wisely."

- Thomas Henry Huxley

Just like the argument about what would happen to animals if we stopped eating them, the economy argument is based on the idea that everyone would go vegan overnight. Obviously this wouldn't be the case. It will be a gradual process that will take decades, maybe even centuries. In this time, government subsidies could be moved away from expensive meat and dairy production, and given to farmers and producers that produce plant based foods.

We are propping up the dairy industry with subsidies to keep it afloat rather than letting it fail, as any other failing business or industry would. Without these subsidies, dairy farmers would not be able to meet the prices dictated by supermarkets and so one of two things would happen: Milk prices would go up and people would be forced to buy the cheaper soy, coconut, rice, or almond alternatives, or, the farmers would go out of business or be forced to produce the more popular and cheaper products themselves.

Given that the move from global meat and dairy consumption to global plant based consumption will be a slow and steady process, the farmers and producers will have time to change their businesses to meet the demand. They may even be surprised to see better returns on their investments which is what business is all about after all.

As an adaptive and innovative species, humans can easily make this transformation to a better solution for the animals, our health, and our planet. We shouldn't be held back by habit, traditions, or by doing things one way because that's how they've always been done. This is backwards thinking, and we have to stop it. Just like electric cars have taken a massive step forward with innovators like Elon Musk (who went against the fuel powered monopoly on personal transport) plant based alternatives to meat and dairy can do the same. The move will create more sustainable jobs and will make better use of government subsidies; if they would need them at all.

CHAPTER 42

VEGANS ARE DESTROYING THE RAINFORESTS

"Trees are poems that the Earth writes upon the sky."

- Kahil Gibran

Are vegans and vegetarians the main cause for the destruction of the rainforests because they eat soy products? Let's have a look. When I first heard this argument, from a friend of mine in fact, I went home to find out if this was true. The first place I looked was to the Rainforest Alliance. If vegans were the main cause then surely they would be letting us know? Here's what they said the main causes were:

"Around the world, people are clearing land to grow crops. While people need to grow food, in many countries, there are no laws to prevent people from entering a forest, cutting it down, burning the dry vegetation, and planting seeds. Because most of a rainforest's nutrients are found in its diverse flora, the soils that support so much biodiversity are actually quite thin and poor. The farmers can grow crops in the ashes of burned forests for a few years, but eventually, the nutrient-poor soils give out, and the colonists must move farther into the forest and start over. The abandoned lands are often used by ranchers to graze livestock. On average, six acres of pastureland in the tropics are needed to feed just one cow. People who need wood for fuel also cause deforestation. When timber companies cut down valuable hardwoods in a forest in an irresponsible way, the process usually destroys all surrounding vegetation and jeopardizes the wildlife that depended on that lost vegetation. Illegal logging is also a problem. Development projects like dams, new settlements, highways and large-scale mining and petroleum projects are also leading causes of deforestation."

No mention of the vegan, it seems to be all about the animals, with 6 acres per cow required. Then I went to the World Wildlife Fund. They stated that of the 284 million tonnes of soy produced globally, 75% was used for animal feed. Obviously only 25% was eaten directly by humans. In Europe the percentages were much worse. It stated that 93% of all soya consumed in the EU is in the form of animal feed. It is so high because we eat so much meat! So if we ate less meat then we would automatically use less soy.

So if we take the Rainforest Alliance and the World Wildlife Fund's information as true, it is clear that the soya is grown mainly for the animals. What's worse is that the animals also need land to live on (be it grazing or imprisoned in factory farms) and the animal waste has to go somewhere. Either the animals are moved from land to land to enable the grazing land to recover or the waste is kept in vile reservoirs that leak, overflow, and pollute the surrounding rivers and environment.

The biggest insult is that we go through this whole process of cutting down rainforest, growing 75% of the soya for feed, storing the animals and disposing of their waste (pollutants) then they are killed and sold for meat and some of this meat goes to waste and is not even eaten. Did you know that 20% of meat is actually wasted; not consumed? That is obscene. If cows are lucky (should I say unlucky) enough to be milked for years and years until they are then killed anyway (for burger meat) then the storage and feeding and waste process goes on for a long time.

Clearly, Vegans are not the cause of the rainforest destruction and using this as a reason to keep eating meat is just delusional. Eating meat is the main cause of rainforest destruction and once that is realised, anyone who wouldn't go vegan because they thought vegans were the main cause should immediately stop eating meat, adopt a plant based diet, and put their money where their mouth is. If they don't, then what does that make them?

SECTION 5 - FARMING

CHAPTER 43

ANIMALS ARE NOT HURT IN FARMS

"The question is not, can they reason? Nor, can they talk? But rather, can they suffer?"

- Jeremy Bentham

Sometimes what we believe is totally different to the reality. Animals in the UK and all across the world, are being bred in factory farm environments. When I used think of a farm, I imagined a farmhouse, a single big barn, perhaps a water well, and lots of different animals all living together in one happy harmoniously perfect scene. Unfortunately this is not the reality, especially where factory farms are concerned.

Farming is a business, and like any business, for it to run smoothly and profitably measures have to be put in place. These measures do not have the wellbeing of the animals in mind. Money comes first and the emotions and suffering of the animal are of no concern as long as the product gets to the abattoir in one piece and in 'reasonable' condition.

Animals are treated as objects. They are commodities, stock, for the farmers to process from birth through to death in the most profitable way possible. Animals are crammed in small spaces, not let out to graze, fed a mulch of who knows what, supplemented with vitamins, hormones, and antibiotics. They have their tails and testicles cut off without anaesthetic. They have their beaks and teeth snipped and trimmed in painful procedures. They sleep on metal grates with the bare minimum of any kind of bedding. Male chicks are ground alive in industrial blenders, gassed to death, or suffocated in sacks. Female pigs are forced into metal devices that prevent them from even moving so the piglets can feed from them on demand; they are mere machines to the farmer. Cows have their calves torn away from them hours after birth and the male calves are confined to veal crates, not allowed to move, and fed an iron deficient diet purely so their flesh will become pale in colour and tender in the mouth. The female cows are then forced into a disgusting cycle of birth, milking, artificial insemination, and birth again. Over and over again until they can't take it any more and are sent to be slaughtered for cheap meats like burgers.

This is going on everywhere, including the UK, and you don't have to look far to find out all about it. The internet is full of resources and organisations devoted to stopping this appalling process. Factory farming is a stain on humanity and we should be ashamed. The only reason we eat animals is because of tradition, religion, culture, convenience, and taste. If we don't need to eat animals to survive and thrive, then why are we doing this to them?

Watching documentaries like Earthlings, or a lecture by Gary Yourofsky, will reveal how badly animals are treated. They are horrible to watch but if anyone wants to eat meat then they should see how that meat is produced and treated when it was a live sentient being. I wish I had seen these when I was in school, then perhaps I would have made the decision to be a vegan many years ago and saved countless lives.

Factory farming is animal abuse on a colossal scale. If anyone says they love animals and are against animal cruelty then they just have to stop eating them. If we all stop eating them, then the factory farms would not exist. The farmers would start to farm crops, nuts, fruits, or vegetables. Over time the consumers would demand cruelty free food produce and the farmers would supply it.

We will explore the argument that not all meat is factory farmed in other sections, but factory farming is the source of more than 95% of all eggs, chicken, turkey, and pork, and 80% of cattle. Processed foods are mostly made with factory farmed meat and poultry, eggs and dairy. Even if the meat, eggs and dairy is not factory farmed, the animals have still suffered and died just for a plate of food that is not necessary.

It's important to remember that the farmers are just like us. They too have been brought up in a world where this is treated as normal and acceptable behaviour. They are not evil people and have families to provide for just like we do. The great news for them is that they can still do this in a way that does not hurt or kill animals, and as we discuss in the Farmers Livelihood section, they can easily go vegan too.

CHAPTER 44

FREE RANGE IS GOOD FOR THE ANIMALS

"You may choose to look the other way but you can never say again that you did not know."

- William Wilberforce

Free Range does not mean that the animals are treated well or that they are having a happy life. All free range means is that the animals are provided with access to the outdoors. It doesn't say how much space the animals have, what the outdoors looks like (i.e. A field or a concrete or dirt yard), or how much time they can spend there.

Often, especially with chickens, the animals can be crammed in a giant shed with only one exit that leads out to the yard. To get to the yard, the chickens would have to get past hundreds, even thousands, of other chickens. If they do manage to do this, they can find themselves in a barren yard full of droppings and with no benefit or opportunity to exhibit natural behaviour such as roosting up a tree or foraging for worms.

The same goes for cage free. Although the Chickens are free from an individual cage, they are kept in a giant cage with tens of thousands of other chickens. These cage free birds are not able to go outside at all, and their miserable existence within a giant building sees them manipulated with feeding and lighting so they produce eggs more frequently.

Profit is always put before the animals welfare and the farmers and producers will always work close to the minimum requirements. You only have to read the UK's government 'Code of Recommendations for the Welfare of Livestock' to realise this country (and most others; probably all others) is guilty of animal cruelty. Just because a set of government guidelines says the practices are not cruel, it doesn't mean that is the case.

Just like the previous chapter (I can't help but repeat it here), free range animals still suffer. Pigs have their tails and testicles cut off without anaesthetic and their teeth are snipped or ground. Chickens have their beaks trimmed in a painful procedure by hot blade or infrared laser. Animals sleep on metal grates with the bare minimum of any kind of bedding. Male chicks are ground alive in industrial blenders, gassed to death, or tossed in large sacks by the thousand and suffocated. Female pigs are forced into metal devices that prevents them from even moving, so the piglets can feed from them on demand; they are mere machines to the farmer. Cows have their calves torn away from them hours after birth and the male calves are confined to veal crates (also called hutches), not allowed to move around, and fed an iron deficient diet, purely so their flesh will become pale in colour and tender in the mouth. The female cows are then forced into a disgusting cycle of birth, milking, artificial insemination, and birth again. Over and over again until they can't take it any more and are sent to be slaughtered for cheap meats like burgers.

These poor animals are still only products in the eyes of the producers that breed them for death by execution. Free range, cage free, happy farm, or any other name derived to mislead us in to thinking these animals are farmed with their welfare at the forefront of any and all decisions that are made or processes that are sanctioned. Free range does not equal compassion or kindness and should not be treated as a guilt free pass to exploit animals on a mass scale.

CHAPTER 45

ORGANIC IS GOOD

"Think occasionally of the suffering of which you spare yourself the sight."

- Albert Shweitzer

The organic argument is exactly the same as the Free Range Argument. Any animal product that is labelled organic, only means the food given to the animal was organically grown. That's it. The image of a happy cow in a lush green field is misleading to say the least. The organic feed is still fed to animals that are kept in cramped conditions and the organically raised animals may never have seen a field or been outside in their lives; save for the lorry ride to the slaughter house.

Just like free range, organic is a label used to make us feel good about what we are doing. It is a guilt free pass to carry on eating animals and animal products. No animals kept in confinement whilst being manipulated, violated, and killed is a happy animal and no poster or clever marketing should be used to try to convinces us otherwise.

CHAPTER 46

KILLED HUMANELY

"For hundreds of thousands of years the stew in the pot has brewed hatred and resentment that is difficult to stop. If you wish to know why there are disasters of armies and weapons in the world, listen to the piteous cries from the slaughter house at midnight."

- Ancient Chinese Proverb

You have probably found that you hear the following statement often: 'as long as animals are killed humanely then I don't think it's wrong to eat them.' For me, this is one of the easiest statements to address and I think just one simple question is enough to make the person making it realise just how nonsensical it is:

"How can you kill something humanely?"

The answer is obvious. You can't kill anything humanely. Taking a life is violent and gross no matter how you do it. An injection, or slow gassing to death might be a quick and painless way to go, but is it humane? We put our pets to sleep when they get old and ill, even some humans can choose euthanasia when the pain of illness becomes too great for them to bare. But to do this to a young healthy animal - just to eat it - is disgusting. That animal has been raised in a farm with their death planned from the time of their birth. They have even had the date set for their slaughter. They've had no life, no choices, every decision has been made for them and every part of their life has been carefully crafted and controlled.

The act of killing is inhumane, but perhaps you could argue the reason isn't. If we kill because death is asked for or if it frees the person from unimaginable pain and suffering, then perhaps can be humane. It's the persons choice to die or their loved ones make the decision that it is better for them than a prolonged period of incapacitation and unnecessary suffering. But if the person doesn't want to die, is in perfect health, and is in the prime of their lives, who has the right to decide for them other than themselves?

We discuss in the Behaviour and Morality section how there is no moral justification to kill animals for food when we don't have to. Taking a life that doesn't want to be given, is not just immoral, it is inhumane, and so are the methods used to do it. No kindness can be given at the sharp end of the abattoirs blade or the dull cogs of the chicken grinding machine. No humanity can be found in the sacks of suffocating chicks or behind the bolt of the stun gun. Killing against someones will is murder under any definition and Vegans choose to stand up against it. The idea that the words 'humane' and 'slaughter' can be used in the same sentence is ridiculous. No form of slaughter is in any way humane.

CHAPTER 47

MISTREATED ANIMALS WOULD NOT PRODUCE MILK AND EGGS

"If slavery is not wrong, nothing is wrong."

- Abraham Lincoln

Animals want to live, just like we do. Whenever humans have been enslaved, imprisoned, held in concentration camps, or exploited they survive through their desire for life. All animals have this, so the idea that animals will not reproduce, lay eggs, give milk, or grow, is a total red herring.

Chickens are manipulated through the use of lighting in their environment to trick their hormonal system. When their eggs are taken, they think they have to lay more. Cows are kept in cycles of pregnancy so they keep lactating. Everything that is done to these animals is a disgusting orchestra of pain, manipulation, fear, and control.

Weaker animals are kept alive through the addition of antibiotics and supplements in their feed and over the generations, their genes have been manipulated to give us the domesticated livestock we see today. I hate the word 'livestock'. It just sums up what an animals life means to the farmers. They are just stock, commodities, objects of a certain value; nothing more.

Most animals are killed when they are still very young. They would ordinarily live for many years, even decades if left alone, but instead are killed when they are only a few months or years old. Even if they were allowed to, most animals would probably not live to their natural life spans due to the harsh environment and conditions they have to endure.

The reality is that some animals do die premature deaths regardless of the measures put in place to keep them alive in the appalling situations they find themselves in. Chickens and turkeys legs can break under their own weight, just because they are bred to have such heavy and oversized breasts. They can't make it to the water or feed and so die slowly and painfully. In fact, most factory farmed turkeys cannot breed naturally as they are too big, so they have to be artificially inseminated.

Tens of Billions of animals are killed each year for food. Of these numbers, many die before they make it to the slaughterhouse and are tossed away as rubbish in skips or left to lay dead amongst their fellow creatures for hours and even days, before being heartlessly discarded and treated as an expected loss. We never hear about these losses, we only hear about the stronger animals that survive the living hell and meet their deaths at the hands of the slaughterhouse worker.

There are many videos taken from animal activists filming the transport lorries taking the animals to their executions. I have taken some myself. You see the terrible condition of them, dehydrated and covered with abrasions and open wounds. They have survived their ordeal only to be rewarded with a gruesome death.

So unfortunately an animals ability to produce milk or eggs is not a product of a loving relationship they share with their oppressor. Animals are forced to produce milk and eggs by a gross cocktail of gene manipulation, breeding, feeding, and environmental control, as well as their innate desire for life.

CHAPTER 48

GRATEFUL FOR THE ANIMALS SACRIFICE

"Indulgence in animal killing for the taste of the tongue is the grossest kind of ignorance."

- Bhagavad-gita 14.16, Srila Prabhupada

To be grateful for something we have received, implies the thing we receive has been given - even gifted - to us. So are the animals wilfully giving us their milk, eggs, fur, and wool? Are the animals marching themselves boldly into the slaughter houses to give up their lives so that we can enjoy a bucket of chicken or a burger? Obviously the animals have no choice, so to say we are grateful for 'receiving' their flesh, is just like saying we are grateful that the slave we owned picked their days quota of cotton for us. Even though the slave would be chained up and beaten if they didn't.

Hunting an animal and then thanking them for 'giving' their life is truly repulsive. If we need to hunt to survive and thrive then the idea of appreciating the animal is very important but we must recognise the animals life had to be taken, not given. But, the majority of the worlds population does not have to hunt for survival, so arguing that hunting is necessary at all, is unjustified both morally and from necessity.

When we think that an animal has sacrificed themselves for us, we take away the reality of the way the animal was farmed and killed. We remove any reality from the situation as well as any guilt we may feel for killing the animal in the first place. The traditions and habits that we have carried through the generations, all make the idea of unnecessary pain and death normal. Eating animals should not be thought of as normal, and it is certainly not natural or necessary, so we need to shake off these old traditions and remove the mental shackles we have been conditioned to wear for so long.

If I can show any gratitude, then I am grateful that we no longer have to kill and eat animals to survive. I am grateful that we can all evolve into compassionate and kind human beings. I am grateful that we are in a position to make a positive change to ourselves, our families, the animals, and the world we share with them. I am grateful for the opportunity to go vegan.

CHAPTER 49

ANIMALS DON'T KNOW WHAT'S HAPPENING TO THEM

"People must have renounced, it seems to me, all natural intelligence to dare to advance that animals are but animated machines.... It appears to me, besides, that [such people] can never have observed with attention the character of animals, not to have distinguished among them the different voices of need, of suffering, of joy, of pain, of love, of anger, and of all their affections. It would be very strange that they should express so well what they could not feel."

- Voltaire

This is a terrible way to justify eating the flesh of animals when we don't have to. Could we go around shooting people in the head and eating them if they didn't feel it or know what we were about to do? Would it be ok to slice the throat of a stranger if we made it a surprise for them? Breeding animals purely to kill and eat them is the ultimate in premeditation. When they are born, the animals have their day of execution booked in. The supermarkets know when they will be received and the butcher knows when their corpses will be delivered ready to portion up. Their only destiny is death at the hand of humans in the abattoirs and slaughter houses around the world. They have no way of escaping this.

This level of death can in no way be justified by the fact the animals have no idea what is going to happen to them. During the lead up to their inevitable death by execution, the animals endure unimaginable ordeals. Families torn apart, rape, confinement in cramped conditions, over feeding, abuse and exploitation on a huge scale. They know all these things are happening to them throughout their unnaturally short lives, and feel every degree of pain inflicted on them. To say they do not know, is to show a complete ignorance and disregard for other sentient beings.

Animals are self aware and much more intelligent than we give them credit for. They are affectionate, loyal, and even compassionate. Pigs are more intelligent than dogs, yet we treasure one as 'mans best friend' and abuse the other, placing our bacon sandwich above their life. Pigs are more intelligent than a 3 year old human child, if intelligence is a measure of how we can treat sentient beings, can we eat them too?

The animals suffer depression, fear, and despair during the farming process. They are forced into the slaughter houses one behind the other and hear the screams and smell the blood of their fellow creatures who have gone in line before them. The end for these animals is in no way a humane process. Shooting a living, breathing, feeling, sentient being in the head with a bolt gun, or electrocuting it before slicing their throat, is in no way a calm or humane process that the animal would not be aware of.

The lengths we can all go to in order to keep the status quo, is morose. We all know animals feel pain and experience suffering. Because we do not think about where our meat comes from and name it beef and pork instead of cow and pig, we have commodified the lives of animals. They mean nothing more than a way to feed our gluttonous hunger for traditional, fast, cheap, and convenient food.

There is good news though. The connection can be made. After all, most vegans were meat eaters at one stage in their lives too. More and more people are starting to realise the meat they eat is the flesh of another animal. The connection is being made faster and in more numbers than ever before and the vegan movement is the fastest growing social justice movement in the world. We can show that meat is murder and give everyone an alternative and compassionate solution.

CHAPTER 50

FARMERS OUT OF WORK

"It is difficult to get a man to understand something, when his salary depends on his not understanding it."

- Upton Sinclair

What about farmers? This is a really important question. I believe that farmers are not our enemy. The system is our enemy. We have all - farmers included - been brought up to believe we need eggs, meat, and dairy to survive. But, to paraphrase James Aspey, while I sympathise with farmers and their families, their profit should never be put above the lives of the animals.

Farmers have an opportunity to move away from cattle or dairy, eggs or poultry and use their land and resources to produce a different product. Land can be used for many things other than factory farming. Change is difficult and costly, but with support from the government these farmers could be in a position to make a real difference. It is not down to the farmers alone. Consumers have to step up and demand dairy, egg, and meat free products and the government has to make a commitment to back this up. I won't hold my breath waiting for the government but as consumers we can really make a difference.

We have been in a similar position ourselves. We owned a bakery that specialised in celebration cakes. We have used eggs and butter on gross scales. When we made the switch to a vegan lifestyle, we knew we had to change the business so it was vegan. We couldn't do it overnight as my wife and I had have two children to support, so the change took a few months to implement. But we go tot the point where we only made vegan produce. We promoted vegan baked foods and vegan cake decorating online and kept our following. We took a dairy and egg based business and changed it completely to one that promoted Veganism and brought about a positive change in the world.

I am not saying this as an idealist, I am saying this as someone who has been in a similar position to the farmer. We changed our business for the benefit of the animals, my family, other people, and our environment. So farmers can do the same as we did. All it takes is the desire to change and a clear vision of how to.

There are many farmers who have chosen to stop exploiting animals for eggs, dairy, or their flesh. They have turned their farms into sanctuaries, produced documentaries, films, and written books about their journeys. Money can be made in many ways that are not at the detriment of the animals.

If these farmers (some of whom are fourth generation cattle farmers) can change, then any farmer can change. We hear all the time how farmers work 7 days a week, 365 days a year and hardly make any money. So why not continue this amazing work ethic and work smarter, not harder? Put this 365 day a year working mentality towards something that benefits the planet, the animals, their future generations, and even makes them more profit! Why be stubborn and continue working in an industry that benefits from the death and exploitation of other sentient beings?

Farmers can be compassionate people too. They can realise that what they have been doing is wrong, and they can change. The following quote was taken from a video taken on YouTube, from a spoken word poem by a farmers son who came to this realisation himself. Now he is encouraging others to do so by sharing words like these:

"For every piece of flesh you buy, you're paying to breed the next to die"

He knows that the power to change, lies in the consumer and this power can be transferred to the farmers to help them see the light and make the change themselves.

Can we really have a world without meat? When we reach a point where declines in meat, eggs, and dairy is putting farmers livelihoods at risk, they will have an opportunity to supply the foods everyone will be eating instead. We will always need to eat something so the farmers could easily grow whatever that something will be.

Eating eggs, meat, and dairy is causing untold harm to our planet, our health, and the animals. If we take the mentality that we shouldn't stop consuming these things just because the farmers will have to find another way to make money, then maybe we should also stop trying to battle crime and curing disease just in case we put the Doctors and Police Workers out of work?

We can make an immediate difference by choosing to stop eating animals and their products and go vegan. As more and more people are choosing to do this, we are in a position where truly, together, we can change the world.

CHAPTER 51

WHAT WOULD HAPPEN TO THE ANIMALS IF WE STOP EATING THEM?

"The animals of the planet are in desperate peril . . . Without free animal life I believe we will lose the spiritual equivalent of oxygen."

- Alice Walker

The World's population won't stop eating meat overnight. It would be a slow and gradual process. But if it did happen quickly, then we could make a deal. I suggest that meat eaters can eat all the animals that are in captivity right now and then after that do not breed any more. There, problem solved. There will not be any animals left in captivity so we don't have to worry about the problem. The lucky animals that had already made it to sanctuaries could keep the species going so extinction could be ruled out too.

Let's be honest, this will obviously never happen in this manner. The move from a world that eats meat, to one that eats plant based, will take decades, maybe even a century or more. For it to happen, the vegan alternatives to meat will have to offer a more profitable option for large corporations to adopt. This is starting to happen right now. The massive French dairy company Danone, has purchased the milk alternative company Alpro. Tyson Foods (the largest meat producer in the US, with products on 2 out of every 5 plates) has purchased a 5% share in Beyond Meat, a non meat protein company that has big plans to help the animals, our health, and the planet.

You may have mixed emotions on meat and dairy companies investing in vegan alternative producers, but to take a positive angle, I think that when companies like Tyson Foods see the potential in non-meat alternatives, it's a step towards plant based and a step away from meat. As vegans, we may not like the choice of investors, but at least vegan products are going mainstream more and more now and the vegan message is being heard by a lot more people than ever before.

How else will the move from meat to plant based go? Regrettably, it will never happen over night but rather will be a slow process over decades with demand influencing supply. If we can keep growing the demand for vegan alternatives then the supply will grow with it. Suppliers on the scale of Tyson Foods and Danone really don't care what they are supplying, as long as they make a profit for their shareholders.

Plant based food production can gradually take the place of meat production and can easily provide enough food for the population and even solve world hunger. If the worlds population carry on eating meat at the current rate and countries like India and China adopt a standard western diet, we just wont be able to provide enough meat anyway. An alternative is needed now, so let make that a vegan one.

CHAPTER 52

FARMERS DON'T HURT THEIR ANIMALS

"If [man] is not to stifle his human feelings, he must practise kindness towards animals, for he who is cruel to animals becomes hard also in his dealings with men. We can judge the heart of a man by his treatment of animals."

- Immanuel Kant

I am sure that most farmers would never hurt the animals they rape, confine, exploit, and eventually send off to be killed by a bolt to the head and a sharp knife to the throat. I just can't accept that giving animals a name and showing them some kindness by tickling their ear or patting their head, in any way makes up for the harm caused to them. We have been so entrenched in the lies fed to us for so many years that we don't even see the exploitation going on right in front of us, or even by us.

Artificially inseminating the animals is a violation, it is cruel. Confining animals in a small shed is cruel. Taking the young away from the mother is cruel. Throwing animals in a skip because they are useless and can offer no profit is cruel. Grinding male chickens to death is cruel. Cutting beaks, tails, testicles, and teeth - without anaesthetic I might add - is cruel. Veal production is cruel. Killing animals for food that we don't need to eat, is cruel.

Steven Weinberg once said:

"With or without religion, you would have good people doing good things and evil people doing evil things. But for good people to do evil things, that takes religion."

I believe that the years of propaganda from the meat, egg, and dairy industries have created a kind of religion all around eating meat and animal products. Dead animal flesh is part of all our most treasured celebrations. Christmas, Thanks Giving, even birthday cakes with eggs and dairy products in them. When good people are brought up thinking bad things are normal and acceptable, they think they are doing good. But when you realise the things you are doing are very bad, once you make the connection, the veil of lies quickly slips away and the true horror is revealed.

While I believe farmers are not the enemy, I think we have to say things exactly as they are. All animal farming methods, whether it be free range, organic, or factory, are cruel and they all result in the same end for the animals. All the animals are killed inhumanely in the same slaughter houses. Any harm, cruelty, or death, is unacceptable, no matter how much the farmers 'love' their animals.

CHAPTER 53

ANIMALS ARE BETTER OFF IN A FARM

"Better starve free than be a fat slave."

- Aesop

Most animals that are farmed for meat, eggs, and dairy would not exist in the wild. Humans have manipulated them over generations, favouring those that produce more milk, yield more flesh, or put on weight faster. A wild boar is totally different to a domesticated pig and a wild chicken totally different to a domestic chicken.

Their animal counterparts in the wild are free to roam, feed, and explore their natural environment. They can interact with their fellow creatures and display natural behaviours. They can breed naturally, eat naturally, and live naturally with a fighting chance to survive. No one is manipulating them over generations to make a greater profit and no one single predator is imprisoning and killing them in the billions each year as we are doing with farmed animals.

Of course, if you let a domesticated farmed pig out into the wild there is a good chance they would not last long. But why would anyone do that? No one is even suggesting it should happen. To suggest that it is better for the farmed animals to remain in farm 'care' rather than be in the wild has no foundation. The farmed animals were never wild and are artificially bred so they could exist at all. If we stopped breeding animals just to kill and eat them, then this false argument about being better off in a farm would not exist.

We have not saved the animals from the wild and given them sanctuary in our farms. We have manipulated, imprisoned, and enslaved entire species, putting our health and the health of the planet in jeopardy in the process. Causing abuse and pain on a gigantic scale with the justification that this would be better for the animals than living in the wild, when they would never exist in the wild in the first place, is a ridiculous argument and laughable if it wasn't so serious and horrific.

CHAPTER 54

HUMANELY RAISED IS GOOD

"There is no difference between the pain of humans and the pain of other living beings, since the love and tenderness of the mother for the young are not produced by reasoning, but by feeling, and this faculty exists not only in humans but in most living beings."

- Moses Maimonides

Can a process of artificial insemination, confinement, and eventual execution ever be humane? What makes a process that ends in a calculated and pre-programmed death by execution humane?

The idea that free range farms are better than factory farms is not always true. Some free range farms are really factory farms with a happy hen painted on the walls and vans. Some free range hens never leave the sheds they are raised in. Even though there is a door that leads to a barren yard, they stay inside, confined by their own conditioned instincts and territorial nature. They are fed organic food, but this isn't in a natural form. It is still in a feed or mulch or pellets, the ingredients have just been grown organically before being processed into the convenient food required to fatten them up for slaughter.

All the acts of disfigurement still occur on free range, organic, happy farms. As we detail in the section about factory farming not hurting animals, they still have their tails and testicles cut off without anaesthetic. They have their beaks and teeth snipped and trimmed in a painful procedure. They sleep on metal grates with the bare minimum of any kind of bedding. Male chicks are ground alive in industrial grinders, gassed to death, or suffocated in sacks. Female pigs are forced into metal devices that prevent them from even moving, so the piglets can feed from them on demand; they are mere machines to the farmer. Cows have their calves torn away from them hours after birth and the male calves are confined to veal crates, not allowed to move, and fed an iron deficient diet, purely so their flesh will become pale in colour and tender. The female cows are then forced into a disgusting cycle of birth, milking, artificial insemination, and birth again. Over and over again until they can't take it any more and are sent to be slaughtered for cheap meats like burgers or ground beef.

This is not a humane way to raise animals and I don't think anyone can argue otherwise. Free range farms may be better than factory farming, but it's just like saying being set on fire with petrol is better than being set on fire with chip fat. Both are incredibly cruel and painful and no way to treat a living, breathing, emotional, sentient being. Just because one way is better than another, doesn't mean either way is good or acceptable.

So what about the best farm life that an animal could encounter? Imagine the childhood image of a farm, with just a few cows, pigs, geese, ducks, and sheep, all living in perfect harmony with acres of space to run and eat in. Would this be humane? I argue it is not for a number of reasons. First, a farm is a business, and businesses have to make money to survive. Our childhood farm would not make money, so no farmer in their right mind would set up their business like this. It would fail very quickly. Second, the animals would still have to be killed to provide the product the farmer sells. The farmer doesn't sell contentment for the animals, the farmer sells the animals milk, periods (eggs), skin, fur, hair, flesh, and organs. As crude as that sounds, that's the reality. You cannot have milk without birth, so cows would have to have young. Male calves serve no purpose or profit, so where would they go? Male chickens the same. You see that an ideal farm is just a dream that, however nice it seems on the surface, is still a nightmare for the animals.

The argument that animals raised on free range farms have a 'good life' is one that I hear often. Free range happy hens produce the best eggs. Grass fed cows are happy and good for us to eat. Free range pigs have a great time rooting around the woodland. These are all things that I used to believe myself. In fact, at one time in my business, I sourced meat and eggs from a local farm where all the animals where raised free range. They had lots of room and were free to roam around and explore their environments. I even went on a tour of the farm and believed that the animals had a 'good life'. I am ashamed to say it now but when I used to eat the sausages I felt justified that this was ok and the best way to eat them. 'The best way.' I can't believe I used to think like that.

It is important for me to remind myself of this fact rather than forget it and get up on my high horse and reign down chastisement on the meat eaters all around me. I was one of them once, and perhaps you were too. This is why I feel so strongly about approaching the subject of Veganism in an informed, logical, and positive way. There are many resources out there that show the horror of the reality of farming, so we do not need to repeat it. We can provide the reference points and encourage people thinking about Veganism to look there and experience the reality. We can support that with positive information, the truth, and positive methods to change their lifestyle.

CHAPTER 55

IT'S HAD A GOOD LIFE

"Cruelty to animals is contrary to man's duty to himself, because it deadens in him the feeling of sympathy for their sufferings, and thus a natural tendency that is very useful to morality in relation to other human beings is weakened."

- Immanuel Kant

'It's had a good life.' This is pretty much the same as the humane raised argument but I think it's useful to have a detailed list of questions to ask, just to back it up and expand on it. Even the way an animal is referred to as 'it', shows the disconnect between what is a male or female sentient being and what many think of only as food.

To explore this good life idea, let's take a look at what makes a good life for a cow:

Is it being milked three times a day, kept indoors most of the time, fed a mulch of mixed feed or if lucky 'grass fed'?

Would cows naturally eat grass or would they eat leaves and other foliages?

Would cows naturally receive antibiotics, B12 supplements, and other vitamins?

Would cows be constantly kept in cycles of pregnancy to keep the milk flowing?

Would cows be bred and manipulated to produce unnaturally high yields of milk?

Would cows have a persons arm forcefully inserted into them to artificially impregnate them?

Would cows be separated from their young only a few hours after giving birth?

Would male calves be shot in the head after birth or kept in cruel veal crates (now called hutches) and made iron deficient to produce pale, tender meat?

Would cows be sold for burger meat when they get too old to produce enough milk to pay for their "good life"?

I would say that being kept as a milk slave only to be slaughtered when their production levels don't meet the farmers demand, is not a good life. Even if they have been lucky enough to be allowed to eat grass in a field, it is not enough.

And would you drink dog milk? Elephant milk? What about pigs milk? No? Then why is cows milk in any way acceptable? Why are we the only adult mammals to continue with breast feeding throughout our entire adult life, and worse, we breast feed from another animal!? No matter how you look at it we are breastfeeding, and breastfeeding from another animal that produces milk to make a calf grow to over 400 pounds in weight as quickly as possible!

We live in a messed up world when people are openly disgusted with women naturally breastfeeding their babies but feel drinking the milk from a cows breast is fine. I have even over heard a group of ladies making such comments whilst sitting around drinking cappuccinos and lattes made from the breast milk of a different animal!

This shows us how much we have been manipulated over the years by the dairy industry. Fortunately, clever marketing is not enough any longer. We can see the truth for ourselves and can make our own informed decisions due to the freedom offered to us by the internet and especially social media. We can show the dairy marketing messages for the lies they really are, and we can dispel this myth that animals held as slaves for our greed, have any kind of good life whatsoever.

SECTION 6 - VEGAN MYTHS

CHAPTER 56

VEGANISM IS A RELIGION

"If a man earnestly seeks a righteous life, *his first act of abstinence is from animal food.*"

- Leo Tolstoy

By it's very nature, Veganism is altruistic. Vegans do not do what they do because an ancient book tells them to. There is no Vegan God, saviour, or prophet. Vegans do not belong to an order or attend a church led by a hierarchy of any kind and they don't have leaders or high priests.

Being a vegan is a true personal choice made to promote compassion and love for all animals. The act of not eating animals or using animal products is all that is required to be a vegan. You don't have to go through a ceremony, be christened or baptised, attend mass, or swear allegiance to anyone or anything. You only have to decide to not participate in the unnecessary harm, abuse, cruelty, and murder of innocent animals. Believing that the unnecessary harm of animals is wrong, is not based on dogma, it is based on rationality and logic. Vegans see injustice and recognise that any use of animals is wrong.

While Vegans are obviously not religious, we do speak up for the animals and can rightly be accused of being evangelical. There is nothing wrong with this. We see injustice, abuse, and cruelty, and we want to try to stop it. Being an evangelist is a positive thing when you are passionate for a just cause. Evangelists are all around us and they too have nothing to do with any religion. Take Guy Kawasaki. He is a thought leader in marketing and was an Evangelist for Apple. I am probably guilty of this too, I love Apple products, and get very passionate when I talk to other people about them. An evangelist is described in the Oxford dictionary as 'a zealous advocate of a particular cause.'

Passion is a good thing and I'd even go as far to say obsession is too. I'm obsessed with our Epic Animal Quest. My wife Rachael and I have devoted our lives to doing everything we can to help the animals. Having a positive obsession is a requirement if you want to make a change. Vegans are a minority and as so are treated like one. This can have its advantages as most people are keen to hear a different opinion or idea, even if they disagree and ridicule it. That's fine with me, I just want to have the chance to talk about Veganism and how the world will benefit when we all go vegan!

So Veganism is clearly not a religion but we are an outspoken bunch mainly because we have to be to get our voice heard. Vegans are individuals who have all found themselves in the same place without any coercion or encouragement from a hierarchy with ulterior motives. We arrived separately at a place of compassion and want to let every one know where that place is so they can travel there too.

I wish I had someone to talk to about Veganism when I was a young kid in school. If we had the information presented to us just as we had the propaganda from the meat and dairy industries, then we could all have at least made an informed decision and chosen a lifestyle that benefited the animals, ourselves, and the planet much sooner.

CHAPTER 57

VEGANISM IS A CULT

"The cult of moral grayness is a revolt against moral values."

- Ayn Rand

If I am one of a cult that is focused on being kind and compassionate to all animals then ok, why not. This cult of Veganism is all about not killing, not destroying our health, and not destroying the planet. Are these tenants bad in any way?

In order to accept the idea that Veganism is a cult, we have to say that the Carnist Cult is real too. The Carnist cult is cruel to animals and kills them so they can eat their flesh and organs. The Carnist cult thrive on unhealthy food. The Carnist cult is destroying the only planet we have to live on.

If you had a choice (which you totally do by the way) which cult would you really want to be a part of?

Passion based on compassion, facts, and science, could not be further from a religion or a cult. Vegans have made informed decisions about their lifestyle and how they want to live on this planet. Most times, these decisions are made for positive reasons and with other animals - including people - in mind.

We vegans have a moral obligation to let others know the things we wish we had been told and taught our entire pre-vegan lives. I wish a vegan had brought their passion to me years ago so I could have woken up and made the connection earlier.

As with most things that challenge peoples ideas and beliefs, people just don't want to hear about Veganism. They get defensive and don't always know how to react. But challenging these beliefs can be done in a calm and polite way, and if you expect and anticipate the defensiveness, you can prepare to respond to them and put them at ease. People have a mental construct of themselves and if you point out that their behaviour and actions are not congruent with how they think about themselves, they will freak out! It's not a nice feeling to realise you are not behaving in a way that you think you are.

So we are not praying to some divine heavenly deity or worshipping some human guru that professes to know all things. There is no leader or organisation that dictates rules and regulations. We are simply individuals that want to live a compassionate life and treat other animals, ourselves, and our planet, with the respect and care it deserves. This is an obligation that we are more than happy to take on.

CHAPTER 58

VEGANISM IS A BELIEF

"Our belief is not a belief. Our principles are not a faith. We do not rely solely upon science and reason, because these are necessary rather than sufficient factors, but we distrust anything that contradicts science or outrages reason. We may differ on many things, but what we respect is free inquiry, open-mindedness, and the pursuit of ideas for their own sake."

- Christopher Hitchens

I have been hearing this a lot on social media, the news, and in person from people we know; we've even been accused of brainwashing our children. There have been news reports about Italy proposing a law that prevents parents giving their children a vegan plant-based diet and as I was writing this book, this topic has prompted an Italian celebrity chef to call vegans 'members of a sect' even stating he would kill them all! (He really said that, check out the article in the bibliography).

So why such strong feelings against vegans and why do some people think vegans are brainwashing, child abusing, crazy cult members?

Being a vegan is all about living a healthy, sustainable and compassionate lifestyle. This should be a good thing, it should be embraced and I can't understand why so many people are against it. It's difficult to hear so many negative opinions especially when coming from your friends and family who aren't prepared to learn about it. Sometimes they get so irate that they won't even discuss it at all.

Choosing to follow a plant-based diet is not something we as parents decided upon lightly. Before committing to it as a family, we spent a few weeks absorbing all the information we could find, (in excess of 200 hours) looking at research around the positives and negatives of a plant-based whole food diet. We were obsessed with the subject and couldn't believe we didn't know all the information that was so very easy to find. The evidence is clear that it is better for our health, the animals and the environment, and this evidence is there if you choose to look for it. Now we find we know too much. Once you know how appallingly the animals are treated there's no going back, you can't unlearn it! You either learn and act on the information, learn and don't care, or just stick your head in the sand and convince yourself it's not all that bad and don't learn at all.

Being a Vegan is not a 'belief'. A belief is an acceptance that something exists or is true – especially without proof – and is synonymous with faith and trust. Belief systems are usually found in religion, philosophy and ideology, where facts and evidence are not necessarily required for the belief to be held. I am a vegan because I know, not because I believe.

Knowledge is based on facts, information, and skills acquired through experience or education; the theoretical or practical understanding of a subject. Evidence is available that shows a plant based diet is healthy. Evidence shows why eggs are bad, why milk is bad, and how our health and the environment suffer more when a western meat eating diet is favoured. Evidence shows how badly animals are treated in farming and also for entertainment, clothes, experimentation, and so much more. Choosing a vegan lifestyle is not based on a belief, it's based on a knowing.

Being meat, egg, and dairy eaters for most of our lives, we went along with everything thinking that free range or farm assured meant something good for the animals. In fact, most of the meat we consumed probably didn't even come with those assurances and we didn't even consider them. We just didn't make the connection. Now we have, we feel so guilty. How could we let all this go on and worse of all, be part of it?

Accusing us of brainwashing our children is just outright stupid, not to mention really rude. As parents, we all have to teach our children what is good for them and what is bad for them. If we know a plant-based diet is better for them, would we be bad parents if we didn't teach them this? If we know it's bad, why would we still let our children eat unhealthily? The whole idea of brainwashing is crazy, I mean, should we also let our children smoke if they want to? What about alcohol? After all 'everything in moderation' (this is a phrase we find is quickly thrown into the conversation). If something is bad then it's our duty as parents to tell them it's bad, while doing our best not to facilitate it.

The brainwashing really occurs when we are conditioned through marketing and media to eat out at places like McDonald's, think milk is good for us, think chicken nuggets are acceptable, and think any animal can 'humanely' have its throat slit, be 'humanely' ground up or suffocated, 'humanely' have its tail cut off without anaesthetic or be kept confined to a tiny space for a short miserable life.

Is it better to pop some fish fingers, chicken nuggets or burgers in the oven with some chips and baked beans, or spend some time cooking up a tasty, fresh, organic, homemade and healthy meal for my children? I think the answer is obvious. It's really easy to flippantly insult people who are trying to make a difference, but it's difficult to listen to what they have to say and then reflect on one's own life.

So to compare how I feel about diet to say a cult or religion, is just absurd and obviously incorrect. If we know something is bad for our children, eating specific foods for example, is it better to go against what we have learned and let them eat poorly, or should we just go along with what everyone else is doing and pick up a McDonald's? I would argue that it's wrong to not look seriously at the vegan plant-based diet and that you cannot accuse a vegan of brainwashing their children until you have looked at all the evidence yourself.

Again its evidence, I'm not just making this up. It's not an idea I've had or a fad I've come across. The vegan plant-based diet is better for health, the animals, our environment and the future of our children, and the evidence is in place to prove it. Our diet is such an important subject and it has serious implications. It has to be scrutinised and discussed, we just can't be led by the corporations and their powerful marketing skills anymore.

This phrase has always been with me in life: 'It's easy to mock what you don't understand.' I don't remember where I first heard it, but it is very true. Many people do tend to make jokes about behaviours that are outside of the norm. If they don't understand something, their way of dealing with their ignorance is to make the person who is behaving differently feel stupid.

Other people – people I like to hang around with – will ask questions, think about it and then make their own informed decisions based on any new facts and information they receive. They won't rush in and criticize something they don't know about and will only be keen to learn more.

My own theory on this – call it a belief if you like – is that most people don't want to change their behaviours. If they find out just how bad eggs, meat, and dairy are to their health, the planet, and the animals, then they will have to change their ways. If they don't change, then they will feel guilty and then turn that guilt into loathing for people who have made the change.

I personally embrace change, it makes life interesting, but I also understand how difficult it can be. You have to want to change and that's the problem. If people are happy with how they are living and don't question things, then they won't get into a position where they are ready and willing to change.

As I mention earlier, perhaps some people hear something different to what we are actually saying. We might say "we have chosen to eat a plant based diet as its better for our health, the environment and the animals", but they might hear, "you are poisoning your children, destroying our planet and murdering helpless animals by the billions". I wish they would hear the positive message rather than drown in their negativity.

Like Spiderman's Uncle said, "With great power, comes great responsibility". I think that with new knowledge comes great responsibility. Once we found out just how bad our diet and behaviours were, we made a change and joined a rapidly growing percentage of the population who have also woken up to the truth.

We want others to see this truth and we hope that by showing a positive example it will encourage other people to think about their health, the environment, the animals, and the future of our planet. We all look at what our children eat and we all decide what we think is an appropriate diet for them. Vegans just take it a few healthy steps further.

CHAPTER 59

VEGANS TRY TO FORCE BELIEFS ON PEOPLE

"Never, ever be afraid to do what's right, especially if the well-being of a person or animal is at stake."

- Martin Luther King Jr

The only thing being forced down anyone's throat is, unfortunately, the flesh of the animals that were killed against their will. Animals are forced to exist from conception right through to death. Animals have no say in any part of their lives and are forced to participate in unnatural and disgusting activities at every stage of their miserable lives.

Vegans do speak out about their eating choices more than meat eaters in general, but they have good reason to. The animals cannot speak for themselves. They need a voice and we are it. Rather than forcing someone to listen and act on what you say to them, Vegans give the facts and show the reality and ask that the recipient think about it and do what they think is the right thing to do.

All around us there are posters and pictures of meat, eggs, and dairy. Fast food restaurants are everywhere, proudly displaying golden arches and old southern men. Bus stops, shop windows, vans, poster boards, newspapers, online, basically everywhere we go there are advertisements to buy and eat eggs, meat, and dairy. On top of this, the adverts do not show the reality of the slaughter process, only the cooked, seasoned, and garnished dead flesh of the poor animals. All these media forms are acceptable, but if a vegan talks about the true horror of meat, egg, and dairy production, or posts something related to it on Facebook, then immediately it's an outrage.

Perhaps us Vegans are guilty of not understanding why someone who knows the facts doesn't change their diet, but it's hard to keep quiet when someone is openly showing a complete lack of compassion. I guess the accusation that we are forcing our beliefs (which aren't beliefs anyway, see section on Veganism is a Belief) on them is a way to put up a defensive wall. What they are really saying is 'hey leave me alone, I just want to eat the animals and live in ignorant bliss.'

CHAPTER 60

VEGANS USE PROPAGANDA

"The essence of the independent mind lies not in what it thinks, but in how it thinks."

- Christopher Hitchens

How often have you seen a post on social media saying that Vegans are spouting propaganda? In the same conversations the meat eaters will throw in comments such as 'well Hitler was a vegetarian', which ironically is using Nazi propaganda to make their own point ... about ... propaganda.

Propaganda is information, especially of a biased or misleading nature, used to promote a political cause or point of view. Interestingly, the term was introduced by the Roman Catholic Church in 1622, when they created a group of cardinals who were responsible for foreign missions. Propaganda of the highest order! So the word is associated typically with large oppressive organisations, regimes, and governments. We all know the horrific things the Nazis did and the Catholic Church has been responsible for so many atrocities of her own throughout history.

To label a Vegan as a user of propaganda is pretty strong coming from those that have literally drank in the lies told to them by the dairy industry for so long. The fact that a meat eater is so brainwashed by propaganda that they can't see the truth behind most things vegans say is quite telling. Decades of brainwashing are difficult to eradicate, but over time they can be. Social media has opened up a gateway for us to walk down a path of truth. There will be some straddlers along the way, but eventually they will catch up.

As individuals, vegans are not tied to a set of rules, or have a set of standards to work to. Vegans are a mixed bunch on all levels of education and professions. I can agree that sometimes things are misquoted, studies are not used accurately or facts are cherry picked to bolster a point, but who isn't guilty of that? However, the information that most vegans use to argue a point, is actually true. It's factual and the evidence is there to prove it. We don't have to elaborate or lie to make a point, we just have to tell the truth. The truth is shocking enough.

The facts are the facts, though, there is no denying it. Murder is murder. Rape is rape. Slavery is slavery. There is no way around it. So when you find someone trying to use stupid arguments like Hitler or propaganda, try to resist the urge to get into a pointless conversation, or get dragged into their strange world. Remind them that the whole reason you are a vegan is because you disagree with murder, rape, and slavery. You have the facts and facts don't lie.

CHAPTER 61

VEGANS WILL HAVE THEIR CHILDREN TAKEN AWAY FROM THEM

"Injustice anywhere, is a threat to Justice everywhere."

- Martin Luther King

This one we experienced early on in our vegan life. A neighbour who was a retired health care professional told us that our children could be taken away from us because they are vegan! She informed us of one single case where a family had their children taken into care because they were 'malnourished on a vegan diet.' They were working parents, middle class, (as if that made a difference) and they were very intelligent people according to her. She raised the protein argument amongst others and was adamant that this was a bad idea and that we needed to research it.

Before we made the decision to go vegan, we had many concerns of our own and spent weeks researching everything we could find. This book is a result of our research in fact.

This lady had no idea that we had thoroughly looked into our new vegan diet and taken all measures to ensure our children would be healthy and happy. She also neglected to talk about the thousands of children that weren't vegan but who were also taken into care because of malnutrition. This is the problem that we find over and over again. One case will be reported by the media of one vegan person in a decade, but the thousands of non-vegan stories are not mentioned. If they were, the news papers would be reporting on meat eaters being taken into care daily. But when a vegan is involved, it's suddenly newsworthy.

This kind of mild hysteria is not limited to disconnected, retired, and misinformed ladies in Cornish villages. Recently, there were reports that the Italian government were trying to make it against the law to feed children a vegan diet! It seems ignorance knows no bounds.

As parents that only want the best for our children, this question is probably the one that could potentially cause the most offence, especially when you get it for the first time. When the lady told us we could lose our children, we were really offended and annoyed to say the least. So how can we handle this objection without getting emotional and should we even have to deal with people like this?

I think we have to respond to this just as we do all the other objections. It will be much easier if we know all the answers and are prepared to give them in a cool and calculated manner. Her main objection after the mindless statement was the old protein one. Easily handled. You could thank the person for their concern and then ask them the following questions:

How much protein should we eat each day?

Where can we get protein from?
What is protein?
What does protein do?

The chances are that if the person knows the answers to these questions, they wouldn't be asking the questions in the first place! When they reveal they have no idea how much protein we all need, you can help them by letting them know the answer as laid out in the section on Protein in this book.

If they have other objections, you can use the answers in the same way. Ask them questions you pretty much know they won't have the answers to and then give them the answers. Highlighting their ignorance in a nice friendly way, will allow you to keep the conversation going and give you the opportunity to drop a few more truth bombs on them.

You could go on, 'in fact, do you know that eating meat is actually bad for you? The World Health Organisation found through hundreds of studies, that bacon, red meat, and processed meats actually cause cancer?' Or, 'Do you know that the 10 biggest causes of death in this country are all linked to eating a standard western diet that includes meat?' Or, 'Did you know that Vegans reportedly live, on average, 10 years longer than meat eaters?'

Any objections misinformed and opinionated people give you can be handled easily when you have the knowledge at hand. It's easier said than done, but ignore the mindless statements and instead focus on the objection they are giving you. Then use the opportunity to highlight their ignorance, give them the correct information, and drop in some reasons why going vegan is the best option not just for your children, but for the entire planet.

CHAPTER 62

VEGANS WEAR WOOL & LEATHER

"It's easier to fool people than convince them they have been fooled."

- Mark Twain

As a rule, Vegans don't wear anything that comes from an animal. There are some exceptions though. Some will keep shoes or items of clothing that they had before they were Vegans and feel it is better to keep wearing them rather than throw them away. Other vegans can't bare the idea of wearing anything animal related, so it's a choice that each of us will make on our own. Buying any new items that contain animal product such as wool or felt is a different story though. No Vegan would ever knowingly purchase any animal products once they have made the decision to be a Vegan.

In my wardrobe is a green hooded fleece containing 30% wool that I purchased before I was a Vegan. I chose to keep it. What good would it do to throw it away or give it to a charity shop where it may never be used again? I would have to buy a new fleece and that new purchase would come with other implications that could be avoided. I would never knowingly buy another item of clothing that contained wool and would play no part in supporting the wool industry. It's the same with carpets. I used to live in a rented house that had carpets that may well have contained wool. I couldn't rip them up and what good would it do anyway? I can see that many people won't agree with this, but I would rather make sure the animal product isn't wasted and wear it myself, than just throw it away.

But could you say the same thing about meat? Meat is on the shelf, so why not eat it? This is a decent point but, as I have keep finding, one that can easily be addressed. By purchasing animal products, we are feeding the demand so more will be created to keep that demand going. If we buy meat from the shelf, that gap will need to be filled again so more meat is ordered and more animals are killed. If we leave it on the shelf and don't buy it, then obviously it doesn't have to be replaced. Do this on a large scale and the demand for the item will be reduced, less meat will need to be reordered, and in turn, fewer animals will be killed. It is basic supply and demand.

Often, people will defend their meat eating ways by pointing out that vegans wear leather boots. The fact that someone would want to find one detail to try to out you as a hypocrite is sad. They are missing the point of Veganism entirely. I'll be the first to admit I feel guilty about the 30 odd years I ate meat and participated in animal exploitation and I know I have been a hypocrite; and probably still am on occasion. Most Vegans were at some point meat eaters themselves, but by getting to a point and saying 'I will no longer do this,' we can immediately stop contributing and making the matter worse and no longer continue to be a cog in the animal killing machine.

The meat eater who points things like this out often doesn't think that they are also wearing animal products and still buy them. On top of that, they are eating the animals, taking their meat and eggs, wearing them, sleeping on them, exploiting them, and being entertained by them. Vegans no longer do any of these things once they realise the reality of what goes on. If you find yourself being presented with the old 'ooh you are wearing leather boots' argument, challenge the person to find out all about the issues and then look at their behaviour before they try to tarnish the great work you as a vegan are doing to help the animals.

CHAPTER 63

VEGANS LIKE TO BE DIFFICULT

"Conformity is the jailer of freedom and the enemy of growth."

- John F. Kennedy

Vegans are often accused of being trouble makers or as being awkward. Going out for a meal and asking for specific ingredients to be left out of food is not fun for vegans but our reasons for doing so are immensely important to us and the animals.

It's easy for a meat eater to look at an awkward vegan and see them as difficult. They are a 'disruptor' and disruptors in an organised system like our society, are not generally welcome. They show an imbalance in the system and cause people to panic. But the problem isn't the vegan. The problem is the organised system!

No one knows how to deal with a disruptor so they go to a safe place in order to put all the pieces back where they should be in their mental construct that is the world they occupy. It's our job as vegans to calmly explain why we are being what they would describe as 'awkward'. If we can pull out those pieces and rearrange them into an order that doesn't require the torture and murder of animals, then we can really achieve something.

It's easy to mock someone that is in the minority and it's very normal, so expect it a lot! If you know it's coming then it's easy to let it go over your head and not take it personally. Remember that most vegans ate meat at one time and you may even have responded in a similar way; I know I did. When I was a chef in the Royal Navy, I remember all of us chefs getting annoyed if we had to make a specific meal for someone who was 'fussy'. There was always a vegetarian alternative on the menu, but it rarely got eaten and we didn't put as much creativity into it as we would the meat dishes. I even remember us all teasing a member of the ships crew because he turned vegetarian because his girlfriend was. Today I would be praising his decision and championing Veganism!

Society and organisations do their best to keep everyone inline with the status quo. Breaking away from tradition or culture is difficult, but the more people that do it, the easier it gets. Vegans can chip away at the majority, sowing truth seeds as we go, and eventually the tide will turn. Meat eaters may well one day become the minority.

CHAPTER 64

VEGANS ARE ELITIST

"Because one species is more clever than another, does it give it the right to imprison or torture the less clever species? Does one exceptionally clever individual have a right to exploit the less clever individuals of his own species? To say that he does is to say with the Fascists that the strong have a right to abuse and exploit the weak - might is right, and the strong and ruthless shall inherit the earth."

- Richard D Ryder

Elitist, self righteous, judgemental, and opinionated. These are all names that get thrown at vegans. The idea that vegans are elitist couldn't be further from the truth. Vegans want every living being to have the right to life and the right to be left alone to live in their natural environment. We want the exploitation of animals, by humans, to stop.

Elitists are defined as a select group of people with a certain ancestry, intrinsic quality or worth, high intellect, wealth, specialised training or experience. The idea that these distinctive attributes place humans above all animals, and gives them the right to farm and eat them, is an elitist ideal. Vegans take the complete opposite stance and are striving for a non-elitist approach.

So to be labelled 'Elitist' by someone who is a willing participant in an elitist regime, is ironic to say the least. Perhaps I used to think the same thing before I learned all about Veganism, but as soon as the definition is laid out and the idea is unpacked a little, it's obvious that vegans are not elitists.

CHAPTER 65

VEGANS ARE JUDGEMENTAL

"Striving for social justice is the most valuable thing to do in life."

- Albert Einstein

I get this, I used to think so too. Vegans are just hippies right? Out of work, festival going, bare foot walking, scroungers, who like to be awkward at meal times? I couldn't have been more wrong. I feel ashamed of myself for not finding out more about Veganism sooner and for just going along with the stereotype. But now I know better, I am obligated to do better.

When a vegan says, 'I am doing the best thing for my children', the meat eater will probably take it as a critique on their parenting skills and actually hear, 'you are NOT doing the best thing for YOUR children.' Any critique of our parenting style or parenting choices is never received well by anyone. And even if you aren't saying it directly, people can get the wrong message. As is a common thread in this book, it's all about being prepared. A few carefully crafted words can ease the tension and encourage conversation and interest. If you can intrigue and encourage meat eaters to ask you questions, then you are on to a winner, a great opportunity to sow a few seeds and positively promote the vegan lifestyle.

As soon as a group or movement of people realise something is wrong and make a stand against it, people react defensively. This has been seen in history with slavery and child labour. But if it is wrong and we know it, what kind of people would we be if we didn't stand up and make a judgement?

Animals are silent slaves. They have no power whatsoever and no voice of their own to speak out with. Vegans have to be the voice of the animals and if that comes across as judgemental, then you'll get no apology from me. If we were in their position how would we want to be represented? What would we want people to say on our behalf?

For a subject as important as animal rights, it is difficult to not come across as judgemental as the decision to follow the vegan lifestyle is a judgement on society; there's no getting around that. But judgements don't have to be negative. We can point out that yes it is terrible what is going on with the animals, but look at the all the amazing benefits that the vegan lifestyle offers! Just being on the side of justice is a great feeling. Knowing you are speaking for sentient beings that have no voice is empowering and something to be praised, no matter how much other people don't like to hear the truth.

CHAPTER 66

VEGANS ARE EXTREME

"It has been said that man is a rational animal. All my life I have been searching for evidence which could support this."

- Bertrand Russell

Is wanting to stop animal cruelty, needless death, destruction of the planet, and world hunger, whilst improving our health, an extreme stance to take? If so, then exactly what makes it extreme, and if it is extreme, why is that a bad thing? Is 'extreme' synonymous with negativity?

Almost every element of the meat, egg, and dairy industry is extreme, and pretty much every objection in this book shows that. Killing over 150 billion sentient beings, just to feed 7 billion, seems extreme, especially when we know we don't need to eat them at all to survive and thrive. Is wasting an estimated 20% of all these needlessly killed animals extreme too? Killing when we don't need to kill is extreme and obviously extreme in the negative way!

Destroying the Earth's natural resources so that portions of the human race can over eat to the point they get ill and die prematurely, also seems extreme in a negative way. You may have seen the meme going around social media where a man is visiting his Doctor. The doctor gives him two choices. First, he could opt for a triple heart bypass where the surgeons would cut open his chest and saw through his breast bone so they could open up his chest to access his heart and arteries, which will need to be scraped out and perhaps the odd valve will need to be replaced. Or, second, he could go on a vegan plant based diet. The patient chooses the first thinking that a vegan diet is the extreme option! This meme highlights just how far we have gone wrong as humans showing that we would choose to put our own bodies through severe trauma rather than just make a few easy lifestyle changes.

Many scientists suggest that if we carry on as we are doing, the worlds oceans could be drained of life by 2050. If this happens, we will all be in serious trouble. We need the ocean to survive and if it dies, we die. This one fact alone should be enough for everyone to stop what they are doing and make sensible choices right now. Anyone who is a parent or grandparent, should be realising that what they are doing now could very well kill their children and grandchildren in the future. It worries me when people are told these facts but they just shrug them off and carry on regardless. Luckily, not everyone does think like this, and if the vegan movement carries on growing as it is, then there could be hope for a bright future.

I could go on listing every extreme example that eating meat involves and I'm sure you could highlight many of them yourself. I've picked out an example above for each of the vegan trinity; the animals, our health, and our environment. Hopefully one of these areas will be enough to show people that Veganism is not an extreme option, it is our only option.

CHAPTER 67

WHY DO VEGANS CARE WHAT OTHER PEOPLE EAT

"The time will come when men such as I will look upon the murder of animals as they now look upon the murder of men."

- Leonardo Da Vinci

While I am concerned when friends and loved ones get ill, their eating habits and lifestyle are of no concern to me. The liberal in me thinks that everyone should be able to do whatever they like to themselves and their body. However, and this is a major caveat, they should be able to do whatever they like as long as no-one else is affected. No one else. What does this mean? No one, should mean all living sentient beings; not just humans.

If a meat eater declares they are upset because you are bothered about what they eat, you could say, 'I don't care what you eat, it's WHO you eat that I'm concerned with!'

If there were no alternatives to meat, then I know I would still be against the way animals are farmed, but regardless, there are alternatives! Why choose to eat a living, thinking, loving, animal when there are tasty alternatives that are even healthier for you and the planet? It really is that simple.

CHAPTER 68

VEGANS USE COMPUTERS

"The true hypocrite is the one who ceases to perceive his deception, the one who lies with sincerity."

- Andre Gide

Not using most animal products is better than using all of them. There is no such thing as a 100% vegan, after all, petrol is made from oil which is, in part, made from dinosaurs! It is impossible to avoid animal products in the non-vegan world that we live in, but that is no excuse for us to not try our best to avoid them. We can boycott products and services that exploit animals and we can choose to spend our money on food, products, and services that promote Veganism. When demand for vegan friendly products increase, alternatives will be supplied to make sure more and more products and services become vegan friendly in line with the demand.

Take slavery. In the 18-1900's, people were campaigning against slavery whilst still frequenting businesses that most probably had slaves working in them. They were not supporting slavery in doing this, they were just purchasing what they needed to live and work in a world that was pro-slavery. Shopping options were limited, but eventually, as time moved on, more and more businesses stopped using slaves, and more and more people made the decision to shop with them rather than with the businesses that still supported it.

Cars have always been non-vegan, but now Tesla has released a completely vegan friendly car, the first of it's kind. As Tesla starts to take market share, other car manufacturers will follow suit and, over time, we will see an increase in vegan friendly cars and a decrease in non-vegan friendly cars. This is how change happens. Demand dictates supply and as that demand increases, suppliers will change their processes and products to match it.

So what if vegans decided to stop using computers right now? Then we would have to stop using transport, refrigeration, packaging, most electronics, electricity, oil, and pretty much all food products too. Without all these things we could not live as vegans and could not be in a position to make a positive change. Without vegans, the world would get worse; much worse.

Everything has an impact on an animal life of some kind, no matter how careful the process is. Growing vegetables will affect insects, as does walking. The whole point of Veganism is to decide to stop intentionally causing harm and exploitation and reduce the unintentional harm as much as is practical and possible. Often the term hypocrite will be hurled at a vegan, even though most vegans will admit they cannot rule out all animal products. As the proverb goes, 'it is better to be known as a sinner than a hypocrite.'

We have to live in the world we find ourselves in, there is no getting around that. But we don't have to go along with it and ignorantly make it worse. We don't have to ignore all the harm we are doing and put our children and future generations in a dangerous position. What we do have to do, if we really care about the planet and it's future, is wake up, change our own lives first, then share our story with the world and hope that they change too.

CHAPTER 69

YOU CAN'T BE 100% VEGAN

"You can have it all. You just can't have it all at once."

- Oprah Winfrey

For once there is an objection that is actually true! Yes we can eat whole foods and use products that haven't been tested on animals, but we are surrounded by things that either have some animal product involved in the process or have exploited animals in its production. This is a bit like the previous Computer argument.

But does this mean we should not bother? Of course not. Just 5 years ago, the amount of vegan processed foods such as vegan friendly Quorn pieces, or vegan sausages, was very limited. Now there are whole sections in supermarkets devoted to them. The power of the people and the demand for vegan products have driven suppliers to emerge and provide the supply. Simple supply and demand.

This is just one example. There are many products in food, beauty, cleaning, and clothing where vegan alternatives have been created and have become very successful. If we can continue pushing forward, and the vegan movement continues to grow as it is doing, then we will only see this happening more and more.

It is frustrating when things that you think shouldn't have animal products in, do actually have them. Doughnuts in one shop will be vegan (accidentally) while doughnuts in another have dried egg or milk powder in them. This actually happened to me not long ago. I was in a supermarket and the ingredients where not on the freshly baked bag of doughnuts. So I asked the lady and we found they actually had egg powder in them.

This is often the case, and products can include animal products because they are cheap and easily available in gargantuan quantities. Since being vegan, we have found that pancakes don't need egg in at all and cake is absolutely delicious without egg and dairy. In fact I would say it is better, moist, light, and fluffy, and keeps that way for ages.

Some things you would never think about have some link to an animal product. I found out, only this week, that toilet paper can have animal products or have been tested on animals. Before I went out to get some leaves from the garden, I did some shopping around, and happily found that Tesco's own brand - any many others - are vegan. What a relief!

Being a vegan is a statement and an act against animal cruelty and unnecessary animal suffering, that's all. Do we sometimes slip up without knowing? Of course. Do we do it on purpose? Definitely not! Taking a persons positive actions and trying to dismantle them by finding a tiny 'loophole' is a strange thing that meat eaters will do. I guess if they can show you, the vegan, to not really be 100% vegan, then they don't have to be vegan either. This is a strange mentality indeed.

Emphasising the idea that Veganism is all about not causing unnecessary harm, should be enough to take the conversation onto the real issues, such as, if you love animals, are against causing animals harm, and don't need to eat animals to survive and thrive, why do you take part in killing billions of them every year?

CHAPTER 70

THERE AREN'T ENOUGH VEGANS TO MAKE A DIFFERENCE

"The love of all living creatures is the most noble attribute of man."

- Charles Darwin

One person can make a difference, but together, we can change the world. I truly believe this. We have seen it in the past so many times. Minorities are ridiculed, oppressed, and ignored, but over time, as their numbers grow, the minorities can impact the majority, and eventually become the majority. If I didn't believe this, I would not dedicate my life to promoting animal rights and doing everything I can to help the animals.

One person deciding to never eat meat, eggs, or dairy ever again has an immediate effect on the market. It may be minuscule, but every time someone stops buying the something, the demand for that thing is reduced. Now what if I can help 10 people, 100 people, 1000 people, see the benefits of the vegan lifestyle? Now we start to see a very real difference.

Gary Yourofsky, the famous animal rights activist that toured the US giving lectures to high school students, took a trip to Israel. Since his visit, the number of vegans in Israel has skyrocketed and it is the fastest growing vegan population in the world. Gary's words helped to show them the truth and he has made a massive stride forward for the animals. The dairy industry in Israel has been effected and they have started to offer a wide range of dairy free alternatives. The demand for dairy decreased, and the demand for vegan alternatives increased. The market saw this and responded with what the customers wanted. This is capitalism at work, so you see we can use it in our favour.

In the UK recently a large supermarket chain, Sainsbury's, released a number of vegan cheese products in most of their biggest stores. They saw the demand for vegan alternatives was growing and they responded not by trying to stop it or distract it, but by providing exactly what the customers wanted.

Charities are funded by small contributions from many individuals. Those small donations would do little on their own, but combine them in one account and the power is enormous. Crowd funding exists purely by this concept and we even set up our own GoFundMe account to help fund our Epic Animal Quest. It works.

Just because it may seem like there aren't enough of us vegans to make a difference, do not be deceived. Veganism is the fastest growing social justice group in the world and we are making things happen. More people are getting it, making the connection, and the momentum is building.

Even if there weren't enough vegans to make a difference, what kind of person would I be to just go along with the crowd knowing that that crowd was doing things that I just couldn't justify morally?

The vegan ocean is made up of single drops of defiance. Given enough time, this ocean will rise and the waves of change will crash against the societal rocks and eventually, little by little, meat consumption could very well be just a distant echo in a discarded shell.

SECTION 7 - MORALITY & BEHAVIOUR

CHAPTER 71

IT IS LEGAL

"The obligations of law and equity reach only to mankind; but kindness and beneficence should be extended to the creatures of every species, and these will flow from the breast of a true man, as streams that issue from the living fountain."

- Plutarch

Just because something is not against the law, doesn't mean it is morally sound. Laws change over time and as our society moves forward and evolves, so do the laws governing it. In the past, laws made slavery, wife beating, segregation, and persecution legal. Even today, we see laws in countries where it is legal to stone people to death or cut off their hands. In the US, it is illegal to murder someone but legal to execute someone for murdering, so taking a human life can be both a legal and an illegal act in certain situations.

Hitler committed many crimes against humanity, but did you know that many of the acts were in fact legal in

Germany? Just because something is deemed legal, does not mean it is the right thing to do. In the UK you can't legally kill a dog but you can kill a pig. In Vietnam, it's legal to kill a dog or a pig. Countries and governments decide what is legal but we can each make a moral decision.

One day laws may make it illegal to eat meat or certainly illegal to farm animals in a factory farm process. Individuals coming together can force society to change. The Vegan movement is growing and growing, gaining momentum and increasing in power. As the vegan voice grows louder, society is being forced to listen, and over time change can and will take place.

With Ad Gag orders in place making it difficult for activists to speak out against the meat, egg, and dairy industries, we have to make sure we continue to do everything we can legally to stop more restraints coming in. The more people that stand up and make their voice heard in a peaceful way, the more power the Vegan movement will have. Change is made in tiny increments over long periods of time. This can be change for good or bad, so we have to make positive changes whilst standing up against the negative ones.

Morality and legality are two separate things. After knowing everything that animals go through, how can anyone think that it is morally sounds to eat them just because the law says we can? While the law says you can eat meat, it doesn't say you have to.

CHAPTER 72

VEGANS MENTAL HEALTH SUFFERS

"Although the world is full of suffering, it is also full of overcoming it."

- Helen Keller

A study carried out in Australia suggested that vegans are healthier than meat eaters physically, but their mental health suffers as they are more at risk of suffering from depression and anxiety disorders. They are less optimistic about the future than meat eaters too. The study shows a correlation not a cause, so adopting a vegan diet will not cause you to suffer from depression.

Moods are actually affected by diet, and the vegan diet has been suggested to improve your mood in general. The previous study looked at a specific question about the future, not a general day to day mood.

Vegans feel positive about their life choices and their diet. Eating plant based makes you feel amazing, and when I switched from a vegetarian diet to a vegan diet, I felt the positive impact within a few days. I just felt more awake, alert, and active. I felt good about my new life choice and was excited to go forward with a positive message about my experience.

After the first couple of months of watching, reading, and learning about everything the animals suffer in the meat, egg, and dairy industries, I was obviously depressed. I wondered how we could ever change this, how could we really ever stop this cruelty and stop eating animals and animals products. I imagine if I am ever tested for depression or anxiety about the future, I will be shown to be depressed, no doubt about it.

After this initial period of shock and disgust, and dealing with the fact I was part of the problem myself for most of my life, I did start to get more positive. We created our Epic Animal Quest, and devoted our lives to helping the animals. Making a decision to step up and do something about the problems was a huge positive step in working positively towards a better future. I realised that the vegan movement is massive, the fastest growing social justice movement in the world. The move towards plant based food and away from meat and animal products on a global scale will take many years, decades, perhaps even centuries, but together we really are changing the world, one small step at a time.

So although vegans in Australia may be more depressed than meat eaters, eating a plant based diet will not cause depression. Truth will bring with it negative emotions, but it is important we don't put our heads in the sand and ignore everything that is going on just because we are upset by it. That sadness can lead normal people to do great things.

Watching all the horror involved in animal product production, and realising the immensely damaging effects it has on our health and the planet, will of course, cause someone to suffer mentally to some degree. It is no wonder vegans feel anxious or depressed, but I believe this period can pass, and I believe it can lead to positivity. Sometimes we need to take a step backward in order to leap forward.

CHAPTER 73

WHY DO VEGANS EAT FOOD THAT LOOKS AND TASTES LIKE MEAT?

"If your appearance is all people see, they have no respect for your mind."

- Trudi Canavan

Many Vegans don't eat foods that taste and look like meat and you can certainly enjoy a delicious and varied vegan diet without them in it. However, most Vegans were once meat eaters and so have been brought up eating burgers, minced beef, chicken, sausages, and other meat based foods. Making the transition from a meat eater to a vegan can be difficult for some people and if they are so used to eating specific foods, it can help to have a vegan alternative available.

The unfortunate reality is that meat does taste good. Although I find the thought of eating meat revolting now, I used to love meat. I would eat medium rare steaks, bacon, cheese, KFC, McDonalds, basically everything most meat eating people love to eat. I chose to be vegetarian purely because I didn't want to be responsible for taking a life if I didn't have to. But once I learned the truth about how all animal based foods are produced - eggs and dairy - I moved from vegetarian to vegan overnight and can honestly say I don't miss eating any meat or animal products.

Once the connection is made, a craving for something animal based seems totally wrong and for me, the cravings never came up anyway. If anyone does get a craving for say a burger or a chicken nugget, then the vegan alternatives exist for them to stop that craving. As a bonus, these alternatives are really healthy and are often made with non gm, organic, and sustainable plant based ingredients. I must say though, I had a Linda McCartney Vegan Burger when we were in the UK and it was absolutely delicious!

Making the connection and deciding to become a vegan for the right reasons is so important. People who go vegan then start to eat meat again probably didn't learn all there is to know about how the animals are treated. That's why I feel so strongly about being able to answer all the questions and why I think the sales process mentality is perfect for addressing all the objections.

To address the original question though, I think there is a better one to ask. The question should be, 'if there are products readily available that look and taste similar to animal meat but have none of the cruelty or death attached to them, why does anyone still eat meat?'

CHAPTER 74

IT'S A PERSONAL CHOICE

"It is very significant that some of the most thoughtful and cultured men are partisans of a pure vegetable diet."

- Mohanda Ghandi

Sometimes, talking about Veganism to someone is like talking to them about a different religion. When a meat eater gets to a point during a conversation that is uncomfortable, or too close to the bone (pun very much intended), they may well protest defiantly that eating meat is a 'personal choice.'

Initially you might think, fair enough, I don't want to be militant and ram it down their throat. After all, most of the time we are talking to people we love, our friends and family. I felt like this for the first month or so, but the more I learnt about Veganism, the more I realised how wrong so many things we do and say are.

Eating animals is not personal as it doesn't only affect the person eating the animal. It's a personal choice for me to drink espresso or eat carrots. No one is harmed by me doing this (be prepared for the argument for animals killed during harvest or the argument against eating other animals foods etc) and no one is killed. Eating meat is different, because you are not eating something, you are eating someone; that someone didn't have a choice.

The animal is a sentient being. It doesn't want to die and only wants to live in peace and be left alone. A choice to eat meat, or even eggs and dairy for that matter, is a choice to kill another living, breathing, sentient being. That choice is far from personal.

To get past this Personal Choice objection, you have to keep the conversation calm and friendly. You may well have taken the 'personal choice' to eat meat yourself at one point, so it should be easy to relate to how they are thinking.

I say something like, 'I used to think it was a personal choice too, but after researching Veganism, I soon discovered that the choice affects other living creatures. Not only that, it is unhealthy and has devastating effects on our environment, one in which we all have to live in.'

Anytime a decision to do something has an unwanted affect on another living sentient being, that choice is no longer limited to the person making it. You can make a personal choice to stop interfering with other living sentient beings though, and you can certainly choose to stop paying someone to kill animals just for you to eat them.

CHAPTER 75

RESPECT MY DECISION

"Never be a spectator of unfairness or stupidity. Seek out argument and disputation for their own sake; the grave will supply plenty of time for silence. Suspect your own motives, and all excuses. Do not live for others any more than you would expect others to live for you."

- Christopher Hitchens

This comes up a lot in other areas, especially religion. We are expected to respect someone else purely because they believe in a certain God or ideology. It's possible to respect the person with the belief, but the belief itself has no right to such respect. If the belief makes the person do terrible things, then we can speak out against the belief and chastise it. The idea of loving the sinner but hating the sin comes to mind.

If a person decides to follow a certain religion that forces them to kill other people that hold different beliefs, then why should any respect be shown? Surely the right thing to do would be to show it a total disrespect, even disgust, and we should explain to the person exactly why we think what they are doing is so wrong?

The person who wants respect for a decision that causes harm to other animals is not considering the animals that their decision affects. We don't respect pedophiles, murderers, rapists, cannibals, or people who are sexist, ageist, racist, or homophobic, so why should we respect someone who is speciesist? Those guilty of speciesism are guilty of being complacent in rape, imprisonment, mass murder, exploitation, sexism, oppression, slavery, and torture. Their decision deserves nothing more than utter contempt.

As with any belief system, individuals are conditioned from birth to believe certain things. They are surrounded by other people who have grown up believing the same information and often generations will pass before them, all being inducted into that belief system. This happens in all cultures around the world. I have grown up with the belief that meat, eggs, and dairy are essential for our health, and that we have to eat them. This is conditioning on a grand scale, with billions of people all believing the same thing.

So I keep in mind that when I am talking to a meat eater, they are just like I was, conditioned to believe things that just aren't true. I try to be as respectful as possible to the person but I treat the belief and behaviour as abhorrent. I relate to them, start sentences like 'I used to think the same thing until I learned xyz' or 'I believed that too until I read xyz'. This is why it's so important to have the answers ready and to be able to reflect on how you felt when you discovered them for the first time.

Giving the person something to think about and providing credible sources for them to verify the information, are two key steps in helping them to break away from the tradition and generations of conditioning. Being vegan is beneficial to their health, their families health, the environment, and the animals, so when you talk about Veganism and disrespect the lies they have been told, you are helping them and doing the right thing. If you took their advice to just respect their decision, then you are turning your back on an opportunity to further the vegan movement and giving them a 'get out of jail free' card to carry on eating the animals.

CHAPTER 76

HUMANS ARE MORE IMPORTANT THAN ANIMALS

"It should not be believed that all beings exist for the sake of the existence of man. On the contrary, all the other beings too have been intended for their own sakes and not for the sake of anything else."

- Moses Maimonides

Are humans really more important than animals in the mind of a typical western meat eater? Most households have a pet, and most of these are loved members of the family. I wonder if, given the choice, someone would kill and eat their much loved pet to save the life of a human they didn't know. Would they eat their labrador if the act of killing and eating it saved the life of someone like Sadam Hussein or Hitler? The chances are they wouldn't do it and so the idea that humans are more important than animals is easily dismantled with this one simple - albeit rather odd - scenario.

Putting animals on a scale like this is not a productive exercise though, and it would be much better not to have a scale at all. Just treat all living creatures with the same respect and compassion. 'What if' scenarios take away from the real life scenarios playing out right now, so as powerful as they may be, they aren't always useful to further the debate or move progress forward.

We seem to have evolved to believe we are the centre of the universe. The idea of being superior to every other living creature is one that has been reinforced throughout time by religion and tradition. This ties in with the section on elitism, the idea that we are privileged and well within our rights to exploit all living creatures that aren't human.

Our idea that we are the most important animal on the planet has led to destruction on massive scales. Forests - the lungs of our planet - are being cut down at an unimaginable rate. The oceans are being drained of life. Pollution is off the charts. Entire animal species are being wiped out every day because of human behaviour. Thinking that we are superior has resulted in us walking a path that will only lead to self destruction.

The good news is we can change our way of thinking. We can change our behaviour. The more people that realise what is going on and see the benefits of a vegan lifestyle, the better chance we will have for a bright future for generations to come. If we want to give our children, and their children, a chance to live healthy and sustainable lives, then we have to act now and we have to act in unison. The vegan movement is so important in changing the human paradigm towards realising we are only part of a complex ecosystem and not it's master.

CHAPTER 77

WHAT ABOUT HUMAN SUFFERING?

"Life is life - whether in a cat, or dog or man. There is no difference there between a cat or a man. The idea of difference is a human conception for man's own advantage."

- Sri Aurobindo

Vegans are against all suffering for any animal, including humans. Caring about what happens to animals doesn't mean we stop caring about what happens to humans. Humans are animals too, but the human animal has one thing that none of the other animals have, a voice. The animals need someone to speak for them and that's why vegans speak up so passionately on their behalf. Imagine if humans were being treated as animals are? There would be an outrage globally, and NATO and the UN would no doubt act to stop it.

Humans do suffer in appalling ways, ways that I could never imagine, but I can imagine and even see first hand, exactly what is happening to billions of animals each year. Most importantly, I can actually do something to stop this happening to them. As soon as I went vegan, I made a tiny, minute difference. Spreading the vegan message, promoting compassion, and dedicating my life to helping animals is something I can do to make a positive change in the world.

Now this doesn't mean I will ignore all the suffering endured by other humans or that I favour one species over another, of course not. I just recognise that the animals need our help and not enough people are rallying to their call.

It is against the law in most countries to hurt animals. Animal abuse is frowned upon and no normal person would intentionally hurt an animal in any way. Yet breeding animals in cruel environments just to kill and eat them, is totally acceptable. People are paid to cut animals throats and bolt them through the head all day long. This incongruent behaviour results in a society that says one action is both good and bad, acceptable and unacceptable. It is illegal to walk up to a swan in the UK and cut off its head and eat it. The Queen owns the swans, so perhaps a bad choice, but do this to any bird in the street, a pigeon perhaps, and I am sure the police will be called. Yet we do this - and much worse - to millions, no billions, of chickens each year.

In Canada, as I write this book, a lady faces a possible prison sentence for giving a thirsty pig water from a bottle during it's transport into a slaughter house. Death and cruelty are common place, normal and acceptable business activities, but compassion, it seems, is a crime.

Any abuse or suffering that is inflicted on any animal is wrong. Killing any animal (including humans) when we don't have to is wrong. We should not rule out helping animals like pigs, sheep, cows, and chickens, just because humans are suffering too; that would be speciesist. Our compassion should shine across all species and help should be given wherever and whenever possible to whoever needs it.

CHAPTER 78

THAT'S WHAT ANIMALS ARE FOR

"The gods created certain kinds of beings to replenish our bodies . . . they are the trees and the plants and the seeds."

- Plato

Religious people will often use their tradition to justify their meat eating habits; "God put the animals here for us to eat." Unfortunately it is not limited to the religious among us. People embroiled in the meat industry, such as farmers, slaughterhouse workers, and butchers will often use the excuse too. Animals are mere commodities to them and they have been brought up to depend on the animal flesh for their livelihood and to support their families. Generations of farmers empower this belief and so it is very difficult for them to change their mindset. As Upton Sinclair said, 'It is difficult to get a man to understand something, when his salary depends on his not understanding it.' Difficult, yes, but not impossible!

Now we don't need to get into a debate about the existence of God here, but this same excuse has been used to justify slavery, homophobia, sexism, oppression, rape, murder, torture, genocide, and much, much more. Basically, religious texts can be used to justify the worst actions humans are capable of, as well as the best ones. Over time though, common sense and morality have shown us that the once barbaric religious acts were disgraceful and immoral to say the least.

If there is a god, and if that god wants us to eat the animals he/she/it created, then why is the process so horrible? Why not just create a nice simple food that doesn't involve any suffering for any animal and doesn't require any animal to be murdered? Oh wait, there are such foods available; plants!

Any god that creates beautiful sentient, loving, creatures, then allows us to do what we have done to them (and are still doing), cannot be a good, kind, loving, god. Can anyone really say that god wants us to slaughter the animals by their billions in factory style slaughterhouses? If their god does, then these slaughterhouses are nothing more than places of sacrifice for it's followers to bath in the blood of the victims. Restaurants, supermarkets, butcher shops, and fast food chains, all must be places to worship in. The cross should be replaced by the golden arches, the crescent by the meat hook, and the six sided star by the blades that slice the throats of billions every single year.

If we want to treat this argument seriously, we have to look at just what the holy books say. The main three religions, Judaism, Islam, and Christianity, all go back to creation with Adam and Eve. The first humans created by 'god' were in fact, vegans! They lived in the Garden of Eden (or, Garden of Vegan, as Gary Yourofsky likes to call it) and ate a plant based diet; except apples of course. Even back then, access to knowledge was restricted by the 'ruler.'

As we stand now, this world is hell on earth for the billions of animals killed each year. Anyone who says they love 'god's' creatures, care about the planet 'god' made, or even love the body 'god' gave them, should pay their 'god' the respect of eating foods that do not conflict with the commandments they so passionately profess to be living by.

CHAPTER 79

BUT I'M VEGETARIAN

"Becoming a vegetarian is not merely a symbolic gesture. Nor is it an attempt to isolate oneself from the ugly realities of the world, to keep oneself pure and so without responsibility for the cruelty and carnage all around. Becoming a vegetarian is a highly practical and effective step one can take toward ending both the killing of nonhuman animals and the infliction of suffering on them."

- Peter Singer

Death is not the only way animals are mistreated. Cruelty can come through exploitation and a life of forced servitude. Cows and chickens face some of the worst cruelty and exploitation of all the animals in farming. I go into detail in other sections for each animal and provide resources to back up everything I say, so there is no denying it. If we can show the person making the objection the information and the truth, then it will help them make a better decision for the animals.

Just as I used to be a meat eater, I was also a vegetarian. I used to think that it was wrong to eat meat and if I didn't need to kill an animal to survive and thrive then I would not do it, nor would I pay someone else to do it for me. I doubled up on how many eggs I ate, bought them from a free range farm just up the road from my house, and carried on eating dairy products. I thought I was a hero to the animals; I couldn't have been more wrong.

As soon as I found out about all the appalling things that go on in the egg industry - even in free range organic farms - I literally went vegan overnight. Vegetarians are a step closer to being vegan than meat eaters, so they should most often be more open to talking all about it. Of course you will come across some that just don't want to hear it, but most will. They have already made a dietary decision with the welfare of animals in their mind, so taking them a step further should be welcomed.

Vegetarianism isn't really the answer for the animals, so let's encourage our vegetarian friends and family to research a little further and make more great decisions to help the animals, themselves, and the planet.

CHAPTER 80

PIG ISLAND

"Only the guy who isn't rowing has time to rock the boat."

- Jean-Paul Sartre

Since my family and I chose to become Vegans, we have noticed the 'Desert Island' scenario pop up with a lot. After thinking about it and having to think about the answer so many times, I thought it would be good to put together a response.

So the question normally goes like this: "If you were on a Desert Island and there were only pigs on it, nothing else to eat, what would you do?"

The first few times I didn't give it much credit, but the question presents a great opportunity to make the person asking it really think about their lifestyle. So now I immediately flip the question: "OK great scenario, but what if we lived in a civilised world, where we didn't have to kill any animals, or confine them, to survive? Imagine we could get all the nutrients, vitamins, minerals, proteins, carbohydrates, and fats, from things we could ethically, abundantly, and sustainably grow? Would you still kill and eat animals?"

I love getting this objection now, because this way of handling it is very powerful. I can quickly turn a 'what if' scenario around, and present a real question that is relevant to our world today. The meat eater actually lives in and participates in my scenario, it's very real. How they answer it will define them.

If you find yourself in this position and your friend or loved one are still pushing you for an answer about their imaginary Island, you could go a couple of ways. Some derivatives of this Island scenario place you with pigs, or chickens, or any animal really. I simply say I would eat what ever the pigs are eating. This may not be enough for our meat eating friend, so if all the pig food runs out what do I do, eat the pigs or die? I guess I eat the pigs, hell, I'd probably eat a human if it came to it! In a life or death situation, Pig Man Friday would eat me without hesitation and I would have to eat him if my life depended on it.

Luckily this Island scenario is irrelevant. Being a Vegan is all about not causing unnecessary harm or death, to animals. For me it doesn't rule out killing animals If I had to. If a bear was attacking my child, I'd kill the bear, no hesitation. If a dog was attacking my wife, I'd attack the dog. These are all self preserving instincts that we have to defend our lives. The animals have the choice to leave us alone or attack us. They have to deal with the consequences, just as a human would if they attacked anyone I knew. Being a vegan doesn't mean I am not capable or willing to do necessary harm. However, I would never attack a bear, dog, human, or any other animal that was not doing anything that threatened me, my friends, or my family. That's the whole point. As a vegan I will not cause unnecessary harm or death or suffering to any living creature. But yeah, if I had to, I'd probably eat you!

I had a conversation with my wife one time after watching a film called 'The Road'. If you haven't seen it or read the book then I would urge you to, it's a great movie and a terrific book. Basically it's the tale of a post apocalyptic family. I won't give away any spoilers here, don't worry. I asked my wife what we would do if it was only the four of us left and we couldn't find any food. If we were all starving, would it be better to just end it for all of us, or kill one of us for the rest to eat and then hope we found more food or made it to some safe haven. My wife was clear she would rather us all die, but I'm not so sure. I think that it would be best to eat her. I am naturally physically stronger so could protect the children from any physical dangers better, so, unfortunately for her, my logic would lead to her being the meal. But could we actually do it and could we all live with the fact we all ate Mum? Pretty grim, but it highlights how far we may go to survive. All of a sudden Pig Island sounds like a holiday camp!

After reading tales of ships lost at sea and crews set adrift in life boats, I can understand the horrors people have experienced in the face of death. Drawing straws to see who makes the ultimate sacrifice so their ship mates can survive. Life is harsh, and survival drags us back to primeval acts.

Luckily, the reality is that we are not in any such scenario. We are not stranded on Pig Island, cast adrift on the Pacific Ocean, or forced to eat our family and friends. As we are not in any such scenario, we just don't have to make a decision. It's made for us already. If we don't have to kill to survive then we shouldn't kill! Life is precious and should only be taken as a very last resort, and perhaps not even then.

So if we are living in a world where we do not have to inflict any suffering or death on any animal to survive, why do most of us do it? I did it for so many years, and I feel so guilty about it. The truth is we have been lied to. We have been conditioned for decades to believe we need to eat animals to survive. Now I know the truth, I know I can do something about it and I think the best way is to be able to answer the questions we get from non Vegans in a way that leaves them doubting what they have been told for so many years. If we can sow a seed of doubt in the minds of meat eaters and encourage them to look into the Vegan lifestyle, then we are working towards helping the animals.

'What if' scenarios are interesting, provoking, and sometimes fun, but the big questions should be about what we can all do in the world we actually live in. What can we do to make it a better, safer world and set in place the building blocks necessary for a bright future for our children.

CHAPTER 81

ARE WE MORALLY OBLIGATED TO PROMOTE VEGANISM?

"The assumption that animals are without rights and the illusion that our treatment of them has no moral significance is a positively outrageous example of Western crudity and barbarity. Universal compassion is the only guarantee of morality."

- Arthur Schopenhauer

I can not find any argument that makes it morally permissible to kill animals for food. Now I know that it is wrong and that there is no way to justify it, surely I am now morally obligated to promote Veganism? Anyone who is a Vegan, will probably also feel this way so do we have to make sure everybody else does? If we don't, are we complicit in the immoral killing ourselves?

I know this is close to how religion is spread. Jehovahs witnesses calling door to door, Mormons walking the streets, and Scientologists offering free stress tests in busy city centres. But while these are all based on a belief, Veganism is not. Veganism is a fact based and ethically sound argument against cruelty to animals, harm to oneself, and destruction to the planet we all live on and share with each other. Those three pillars have not been forged by thousand year old doctrines, ancient myths, or holy books. Instead they have been built around sound science, moral and ethical analysis, and well documented evidence.

We all know how wrong it is to harm an animal yet we have got to a point where we don't recognise our food as an animal anymore. We are so far removed from the actual process of slaughter and butchery that the baby lamb we see in the field, has nothing to do with the leg of lamb on our kitchen table. Shrink wrapped, labelled, and placed in a bright clean aisle in a supermarket, leaving no evidence of death and violence behind it.

So why do I think it is not morally permissible to kill animals for food? Billions of animals are killed every year just for food, even though we don't need to eat animals. We can eat plant based foods which are better for us, the planet and the animals. There seems to be five main arguments: Top of the food chain, It's natural, Genetic make up, Lack of love, and Intelligence. Let's look at these arguments.

Top Of The Food Chain

We have evolved to be able to use tools and intelligence to manipulate our environment. This gives the illusion that we are top of the food chain. I argue that we have actually removed ourselves from the food chain altogether, as we would be in serious trouble if we didn't have our technology to hand and had to live in the wild with every other animal; our 'prey.'

Let's say that we are in the top position of power though. Does it make it morally permissible to take advantage of this and impose our will on weaker, less intelligent and resourceful animals?

If it is, then surely we could impose our strength on weaker people and eat them? Should people who are stronger than me, be able to eat me? This seems totally wrong though, or at least I hope it does.

It Is Natural To Kill Animals For Food

This is close to the food chain argument. We have naturally evolved to be able to do lots of things. Some of these things that are natural for us, are actually illegal now. As we have evolved, so has our society and that society has decided that some things, rape and murder for example, are bad. They may be natural, but we shouldn't do them. So if we say it is morally permissible to kill animals to eat them because it comes naturally to us, should we also argue that society has got it wrong and it is, in fact, ok to rape and murder again?

Difference In DNA?

If it is ok to eat other animals because their genetic make up is different to ours, then surely it is ok for them to eat us too? If we try to argue it's morally ok to eat others animals based on genetic make up, then we shouldn't be stopping any animals eating humans. Should We?

How about this next scenario? Imagine an alien race descends on Earth. They see us humans are plentiful; too many if anything. They decide that our genetic make up is so different from theirs that we are, indeed, a different species. We can't communicate with them because they 'talk' telepathically. Our primitive spoken language is far beneath them. They start to farm and eat us. Is this ok? It doesn't seems right does it? But it is exactly the same as us eating cows, chickens, or pigs if we base our reasoning on the difference in our genetic makeup.

Intelligence

Another reason some people claim it's morally permissible to kill animals for food, is the intelligence argument. Pigs, chickens, cows, and rabbits are less intelligent than we are. Some humans hold themselves as superior to animals based on intelligence. So if it's ok to kill an animal for food because they are less intelligent than us, can we eat severely mentally handicapped people? After all they are less intelligent than us too.

Pigs are as intelligent as a 3 year old child. So is that our benchmark? Any human under 3 years old is fair game? Based on the intelligent argument, we should be morally permitted to eat a human if they are less intelligent than a pig. This seems wrong though, right?

Lack of Love

Let's leave humans out of this next argument. How about your pet? If you have a dog or cat, would you kill them for food? No? Why not? What is the difference between a pet dog or cat, and a cow or pig? They are all animals and they all exhibit similar behaviours and levels of intelligence. Their genetic make up is different enough from our own to put them in the food category.

The only thing that seems to separate our cat or dog from a cow or pig, is love. We love those animals. So if love is the barrier between a friend and a feast, what about the people we don't love? I know I said leave humans out of it, but I can't help it!

The love lies with us, so if we love a pig or cow, then that should immediately remove them from the menu. But what if someone else doesn't love our pet, or pig, or cow? Is it morally permissible for them to eat an animal we love because they don't love them? It seems that it is not ok.

No Animal Wants To Be Eaten

I don't want to be eaten. I don't think my Alfie dog wants to be eaten either. If he doesn't want to be eaten, and I don't want to be eaten, it follows that no animal wants to be eaten. Animals move away from pain and they run from predators after all. So if we can agree that no animal wants to be eaten, then we should also be able to agree that the animal thinks it is morally impermissible for anyone to eat them .

If they don't want to be eaten, how can we have any moral basis to override their desire for life and kill them for food we don't even need to survive and thrive?

After a lot of reading and searching, I can't you think of, or find, a single argument that makes it morally permissible to kill animals for food when we don't need to in order to survive and thrive.

SECTION 8 - OTHER ARGUMENTS

CHAPTER 82

HUNTERS TAKE THE PLACE OF EXTINCT PREDATORS

"Though boys throw stones at frogs in sport, the frogs do not die in sport, but in earnest."

- Bion of Borysthenes

We have to ask, why aren't the natural predators there anymore to hunt the prey animals? The answer: because we have hunted them and killed them all. Hunters are claiming to fill a 'gap' that only exists because hunters killed animals and created the gap in the first place. It's just like saying, 'I have to start cleaning windows for a living now, because I murdered all the window cleaners.'

Natural predators and prey exist in a finely balanced tune with their environments. Herds are affected by the amount of food they can eat and predators will be affected by the territory they occupy and hunt in. Human hunters completely destroy this fine balance by first killing the

236

predators, then wiping out the strongest of the prey for the biggest antlers or horns to adorn their walls with. The prey populations are so decimated by humans that natural predators would have difficulty repopulating barren areas of the wilderness.

If the reason to hunt is to take the place of the real predator, then why not work on bringing the predators back, just like what is being proposed with some wolf populations in parts of North America? Hunters just want to hunt, that's all there is to it, and rather than make lame excuses, I would rather they just admit that they like hunting and needlessly killing animals, then we would all know where we stood.

Hunting is not good for wild animals. There is no denying this, so to say that hunting helps keep the population to a sustainable level is pure nonsense. Nature is the best measure of what is sustainable, so if we just keep out of it and let nature do her job, the other animal populations will sort everything out just fine.

Human intervention has messed up so many times. We see it in Australia where animals have been introduced for food and then go feral. Humans then bring in another animal to 'kill off' those feral animals, then that fails miserably and they go feral too! Now humans go out and hunt both the predator and the prey and everything is totally out of control. There is just no excuse to hunt when we don't need to kill animals to survive and thrive anymore.

CHAPTER 83

WE USE EVERY PART OF THE ANIMAL

"Wild animals never kill for sport. Man is the only one to whom the torture and death of his fellow creatures is amusing in itself"

- James Anthony Froude

I'm sure that any animal who has been shot through the head or body would be really pleased to know every part of his or her rotting corpse will be used. Using every part of the animal does not make up for killing them in the first place. If you had to eat an animal to survive then perhaps that's totally different, and using every part is sensible if you were in that situation. But as we keep stressing, we are not in any such situation and we don't have to kill any animal to survive and thrive anymore.

Although hunters like to say they use every part of the animal, this is not always true as most things don't apply to the whole group of any sub culture. Many hunters only take the 'best parts' and leave the rest where it lay. I guess other wild animals and insects would feast on the carcass, but if the hunter is honest, they probably aren't bothered once the prime cuts have been removed. The idea of hunting a stag or other majestic animal to just take a slice of the 'best bits' and then tastelessly mount their head on a wooden board on the wall of an office is repulsive. It feeds the ego of man to highlight how we show a dominance over the other animals rather than a coexistence founded on peace and compassion.

Factory farmed animals use most of the animal too, probably more than a hunter would when you consider the amount of products that have gelatine in them and where that comes from. So using all the parts of something you have murdered, is never a consolation or justification for the act.

It has always baffled me, even before I was a vegan, how people who eat meat disagree with hunting. They think it's cruel to track and shoot a wild bird or a stag, but are more than happy to drive to the supermarket and pick up a nicely wrapped chicken or pack of prime cut steak. The animals that ended up in the supermarket are a product of exploitation, imprisonment, and torture, while the free hunted bird has had the freedom they deserved; at least for a little while. Of course it's not cool to take the life of any animal but meat eaters display a strange level of hypocrisy with this issue and feel that it's better to eat an animal that has been imprisoned and murdered with no chance of escape. The slaughterman's knife never misses the target. As with the dog eating in the Chinese Yulin festival, meat eaters who eat tonnes of chicken, cows, pigs, and sheep, are the first to protest when dogs are eaten. Hypocrisy runs deep.

Most meat eaters are totally against using every part of an animal anyway. When dining out at a restaurant, they could be happily sitting down eating the kidney of a lamb, the congealed excretion of a cow, the period or wings of a chicken, the feet (trotters) or minced eyelids, lips, and bum holes of a pig neatly packed into a sausage, but freak out when they have a hair in their food!

CHAPTER 84

EATING MEAT ADVANCED CIVILISATION

"Until we have the courage to recognise cruelty for what it is - whether its victim is human or animal - we cannot expect things to be much better in this world. We cannot have peace among men whose hearts delight in killing any living creature. By every act that glorifies or even tolerate such moronic delight in killing, we set back the progress of humanity."

- Rachel Carson

It is not just meat that helped us to develop into the advanced civilisation we are today. Our advancements also had a lot to do with slavery and exploitation. If we are to carry on eating meat because it got us to where we are now, then shouldn't we also keep slavery going?

The idea that where we are today is a good thing is also flawed. We are destroying our planet with the things our new found technology has granted us. Oil, meat, gas, coal, and many other resources, are stripping the Earth and placing mankind in a dangerous position. We have developed weapons that could totally destroy every living creature on the planet, and we continue to keep spending to find more and more ways to do it! Rather than invest in solutions to save the planet and stop world hunger, we would rather invest in death and destruction.

I would argue that if eating meat has helped to get us to this position, then we have to stop eating it right now! Regardless of all the other important reasons to stop eating meat that we go through in this book, this one should be obvious and it certainly shouldn't be used as a reason to carry on doing the things that are destroying us.

CHAPTER 85

AGREE TO DISAGREE

"I'd agree with you, but then we'd both be wrong."

- Russell Lynes

When someone wants to end the conversation with, "well, we will just have to agree to disagree," I get very frustrated. Have they even listened to anything we talked about? You can't logically disagree with the vegan argument, that's why it is such a strong case. We don't need to eat animals to survive and thrive. We don't need to wear animals. We don't need to be entertained by animals. The only reasons we exploit and eat animals is for taste, tradition, convenience, and habit.

All these reasons are easily discarded and there are vegan alternatives for each of them. What the person is really saying is, 'let me just keep my head in the sand, because if I listen to everything you are saying, I will feel guilty and will have to change my ways.'

So where do we go when someone says this? It's difficult, but I think we can just keep it simple. We can end with 'ok, but you are against causing unnecessary harm to animals though right?' They will have to say yes to this question and they will no doubt genuinely believe they are against it. 'Then you already think like a vegan. Now all you have to do is act like one.'

I would leave the conversation by asking them to think about what we have talked about and ask them to watch some of the many documentaries out there, like Earthlings. Some people just don't want to change or are not ready to, but we can sow a small seed that may sprout up into a vegan months later. Asking them to follow up in their own time is a good way to get them curious. Perhaps you know them or could get to know them, and then follow up a week later to see if they had a chance to watch or read your recommended sources? The least we can do for the animals is try and do our best to promote a positive vegan message whenever and wherever we can.

CHAPTER 86

LIVE AND LET LIVE

"The only way to live is to let others live."

- Mahatma Ghandi

This is similar to the 'agree to disagree' response in some respects. During a conversation I had with a dairy farmer, we went through most of the arguments in this book and he ended with, 'we should all live and let live.' My immediate response was that that was the whole point of Veganism and why we disagree with each other. I want to stop all animals being killed and he doesn't let them live!

It is so bizarre to have a conversation with someone who is so involved in murder on a mass scale but believes they are doing nothing wrong. Their actions are so normalised, that we are the weirdos for wanting to stop them.

So if I ever receive this response again - and I'm sure I will - I will be ready to point out the obvious. You can't live and let live if you partake in the abuse and murder of innocent sentient beings.

CHAPTER 87

IT'S TOO EXPENSIVE TO GO VEGAN

"The most precious things in life are not those you get for money."

- Albert Einstein

Vegan alternatives can be more expensive than the meat, egg, and dairy versions. Vegan Mayonnaise is a little bit more expensive than a mid level brand and much more than an 'own brand' mayonnaise. But for a little bit extra, you can buy an ethical product that really tastes as good as any mayonnaise made with eggs. No animals have been harmed, and all the ingredients are GMO free, organic, and sustainably grown. This is a lot to get for just a little bit extra money.

But if this is too much, and I get that, it's difficult raising a family or living as a student or on a low wage, then there are lots of options for being a vegan on a budget.

I can agree that Quorn products, Tofurkey, and other such vegan brands are expensive. But you don't have to eat them. We hardly eat any processed brand products like these. With the exception of some sliced sandwich processed vegan 'meats' and my favourite vegan sausage rolls, we easily lived on a whole food style diet in the UK. As I write this, we are in Cambodia on our Epic Animal Quest. There are hardly any meat substitutes and certainly no vegan sausage rolls or vegan mayonnaise. But so what? We just don't have them in our diet anymore and don't think anything of it.

Bananas are so cheap anywhere in the world. In the UK, you can buy 4 for around 50p. Potatoes are literally cheap as chips, and broccoli is 40-50p a head. For my lunch at work I would often eat a whole cucumber, a pot of hummus, a carrot, two bananas, and some pitta bread, all for under £2. I would be really full up after this, and it was all good, healthy food. If you make your own hummus, you can reduce the cost by half!

Evening vegan meals can be much less than meat meals. Take a chilli con carne for example. Make it exactly like the meat version, but leave out the meat and add an extra can or two of kidney beans, mixed beans, or any kind of bean you like. You might like to add a few spoonfuls of nutritional yeast too. I guarantee, weight for weight, beans are cheaper. You get all your protein and everything else you need from the vegan chilli version, but without the animal suffering, death, cholesterol, and carcinogenics.

Seasonal, locally grown fruit and vegetables are cheaper to buy than out of season ones. A good vegan cookbook can help you come up with tasty recipes to make a variety of awesome meals. We wrote a review about our favourite vegan book on our website if you would like to check it out.

As a family of two adults and two young children, we have found a decent reduction in our weekly spend. We used to spend about £100 a week on food in the UK. This was reduced to less than £90 when we went vegan. We buy less junk food, mainly because most junk food has an animal product of some kind in it. We are much more conscious about what we eat and what nutrients we get from different foods.

So in our experience, it is actually cheaper to eat a vegan diet and much more healthy than a standard western diet. Of course, if you buy processed foods and don't cook from whole food ingredients, you will probably find no difference in your food spend. Eating out will be different though, and with your options reduced, you will spend less or at least the same. Most vegan restaurants charge the same as conventional meat restaurants so you will not have to spend any more than you usually do to eat out. Your options may be limited, but your budget won't be.

So you can eat for less at home, for lunch at work, and the same if eating out. Cost is just not an issue and I am glad that's the case. Putting our wallet above the abuse and murder of animals is not a good thing to do, and should never be a reason to justify it.

CHAPTER 88

HITLER WAS A VEGETARIAN

"Never forget that everything Hitler did in Germany was legal."

- Martin Luther King Jr

Hitler's biographer, Robert Payne, tells us that the vegetarian claim was made up by Joseph Goebbels, the Minister of Propaganda at the time, to make Hitler seem like a peaceful man and paint him as a Gandhi like figure. Author Rynn Berry maintains that although Hitler reduced the amount of meat in his diet, he never stopped eating meat completely for any significant length of time. Berry claimed that many historians use the term 'vegetarian' incorrectly to describe someone who simply reduced their meat consumption.

It is well documented, in many books, that Hitler did actually eat meat including liver dumplings, Bavarian sausages, and stuffed squab. These are not just eye witness testimonies from hotel and catering staff, but also from his personal chefs. A book called The Hitler Book, which was prepared by one of Hitler's closest personal aides, states that, "after midnight she would direct [for Hitler] that there should be another light snack of turtle soup, sandwiches and sausages".

Using the, "but, Hitler was a vegetarian" argument, is literally using Nazi propaganda to make an argument against Veganism. So if anyone uses the reason they won't go Vegan because the Nazis used propaganda to falsely sell the idea that Hitler was a vegetarian (not even a vegan), they are very much fooled by 1940's mind manipulation. If anyone wants to be guided by Hitlers behaviour, then how can they justify drinking water? I'm pretty sure Hitler drank that on occasion too.

This argument is really scraping the barrel and is so off point it's not even funny. I shouldn't have to mention that other leaders such as Pol Pot, Stalin, and many more, all ate meat. If the diet of dictators are an important measure to tell us how we should be eating, then surely meat is right off the menu too?

Even if these personal accounts, books, and other sources were somehow not true, and Hitler didn't eat animal meat, and someone wants to stick with this argument, just ask them, how does it feel to know that one of the most evil men in history was kinder to animals than you are?

CHAPTER 89

PLANTS HEAR THEMSELVES BEING EATEN

"He plants trees to benefit another generation."

- Caecilius Statius

This idea comes from a study that found plants have chemical defences that are activated by the vibrations of feedings insects. As is normally the case, the media took this finding and ran with headings like, "plants can hear insects eating them," or, "plants can hear themselves being eaten".

Needless to say, vibrations and hearing are not the same thing and we all know that plants do not have ears, ear canals, central nervous systems, or brains to process information from animal like sensory organs that they don't possess anyway. In short, no brain usually means no pain.

There is no proof anywhere that says plants experience sense data, so they are not subjectively aware. Plants are not sentient beings and so have no thoughts, feelings, emotions, or central nervous system. So as far as we know, eating plants does not cause pain or suffering on any level. Animals, on the other hand, do have thoughts, feelings, emotions, and a central nervous system. Trying to say that plants are the same as animals and vegans are the same as meat eaters because you have read or heard a bogus headline in a newspaper, is ridiculous and insulting. Making out that's it's wrong to eat plants if they feel pain should be taken as an admission that it is wrong to eat animals that we all know do feel pain and so much more.

As far as we know, we are not harming plants and when we eat them we are not causing them pain or taking a life as we know it. When people eat meat, they know (or should know) that the meat they are eating is actually flesh from an animal that once felt, experienced, dreamt, learned, loved, grieved, feared, and experienced thoughts. The dead animals that meat eaters choose to eat were once very much alive and afraid. Anyone with a pet can relate to how much an animal experiences and interact with their environment and other animals. To paraphrase the head of PETA, a dog, is a pig, is a cow, is a chicken, but it certainly isn't a plant!

CHAPTER 90

TOMATOES SCREAM WHEN CUT

"It is better to remain silent and be thought a fool, than to speak and remove all doubt."

- Chinese Proverb

You may have heard the story of how tomatoes scream when you cut them? Surely this must come from a credible source, as so many people refer to it? Well, if you think the dead sci-fi novelist and leader of a crackpot 'religious' organisation, L Ron Hubbard, is a good source, then by all means, believe away.

If you believe Hubbard on this matter, then you may also believe that we live on for billions of years, or that we have the dead souls of aliens that were thrown into volcanoes floating around in our bodies. This guy has no scientific basis for saying that the effects of a metal knife moving within a magnetic field (in this case the tomato's magnetic field) changing the resistivity, is instead, the tomato 'screaming.'

The electric field is effected and, in turn, the electrical properties of the tomato are changed. That's all that happens.

He came to this conclusion after using his E-meter, which is designed to measure changes in resistance of a substance. The substance usually using the E-meter is a gullible human being, but for some reason, Hubbard decided to rig his contraption to a tomato and cut it. So obviously the tomato wasn't screaming and they don't scream when we cut them. And guess what? Carrots don't bark, onions don't cry, and potatoes don't yawn either!

CHAPTER 91

SOY, LABIDO, SPERM, AND PENIS GROWTH

"One dog barks at something, and a hundred bark at the bark."

- Proverb

Does eating Soya lower your sperm count? What seems to have happened is that one study back in 2008 suggested that there may be a link between high levels of soya in a diet and lower concentration of sperm. However, that same study showed that the same participants were obese or overweight. There was no conclusion that stated a link or any proof whatsoever that soya is the cause. No monks participated in this study either, but the click baiters made full use of the tale of the monk eating soya products to lower his labido. Using the monk story in the same paragraph as the study gave the impression the two were connected. They are not connected. The monk story is just that, a story, and the study gave no conclusive evidence, only a suggestion.

We found studies that showed the same inverse relation between processed meat and low sperm count. One study showed the sperm count to be 25% lower in the participants who ate the processed meat. Alcohol, smoking and fizzy soda drinks were also suggested to cause low sperm counts. So the hype created from this single 2008 study continues to misinform people to this day. When you look at more recent studies, the problem appears to be far worse in our standard western meat eating diet.

When you think you have heard it all, you can get hit with new objections like the one we heard about Soy causing young boys penis' to not grow! As we have a young son, this was something that shocked us. We looked online for at least an hour and couldn't find any studies that suggested eating soya over the age of 6 months caused penis' to stop growing! However, it is agreed that infants should not be fed soya based formula and mothers milk is the best. Breast is always best! So the myth that boys penis' don't grow is crazy. The NHS in the UK recommends two servings of soya per day and non GMO organic is preferred. Many other credible sources concur with this advice, and none of them make sensational claims like the one about penis growth.

CHAPTER 92

NO PUSS IN MILK

"The greatness of a nation and its moral progress can be judged by the way its animals are treated."

- Mohanda Ghandi

When I chose to go vegan, I found out that cows milk contains puss. Whenever I discussed this with people who still drunk cows milk, they just didn't believe me. So, to make sure I could back up what I was saying, I went to the actual farming guidelines to get the information that proves there really is puss in cow's milk.

No matter how many antibiotics or chemicals are given to cows, we still find 50% of them become infected with mastitis. This leads to damage to the udders and teats, and the infection causes puss to form and that puss gets taken in with the milk through the milking apparatus. Milking the cows while they have these infections is incredibly painful and cruel. It hurts the cow, but that doesn't stop the milking process. Milk, puss and all, are still taken from her, and more antibiotics are given.

But surely dairy farmers are not allowed to let any kind of puss enter the milk? It seems obvious right? Wrong. Puss is allowed and there are acceptable levels. In a section of the Milk Hygiene Guide For Milk Producers by the Food Standards Agency in the UK, it says that:

"Food operators must initiate procedures to ensure that raw milk meets the following criteria: (i) for raw cows' milk: Plate count at 30°C (per ml) < 100 000 (*) Somatic cell count (per ml) < 400 00 (**)"

Notice the 'Somatic cell count'. This is simply defined as a living cell. Somatic cells come from the puss that forms when infections such as mastitis occur and is purely from damage to the udders. The majority of somatic cells are actually leukocytes which are white blood cells.

So there are acceptable levels of puss in our milk. This in turn, means there is an acceptable level of pain and suffering that can be inflicted on the poor cows. They can be infected and in pain and that's fine as long as that doesn't cross a threshold set by the government.

Now pasteurisation does make the milk safe to drink apparently, but the puss is still in there, it's just been heated to a temperature high enough to stop the bacteria multiplying. Milk has puss and it's not a fact that is hidden. Have a read of the Milk Hygiene Guide For Milk Producers by the Food Standards Agency in the UK yourself, it's on page 24.

CHAPTER 93

FISH DON'T FEEL PAIN

"Our task must be to free ourselves from this prison by widening our circle of compassion to embrace all living creatures and the whole of nature in its beauty."

- Albert Einstein

If something does not feel pain, is it still ok to torture, kill, and eat it? If an animal has a smaller brain than we do, do they feel less pain? Do cold blooded animals feel no pain because they are cold blooded? Does a hook to the mouth really not hurt? Why do fish try to swim away when hooked on line if they can't feel the hook? Do fish really not feel any pain or fear when they are suffocating out of the water during a slow death? Is it true sharks don't feel pain when they have their fins cut from them before they are tossed back in ocean while still alive to bleed to death or slowly drown?

Fishermen and women would say they know the answers to all these questions, but unfortunately they are wrong. We know that fish have good memories and can indeed feel pain. They struggle and fight to survive and when they are removed from the water and they fight to get back to it.

Fish go through a horrible ordeal when out in the wild and we all know by now just how destructive commercial fishing is to the oceans and the fish populations. But even sport fishing is cruel and unnecessary. Catch and release is the name of the game for coarse anglers, and after they have hooked a fish, tired it out, and dragged it out of the water for a photo and maybe a little kiss, they put it back in as if they are doing it a favour. They say they respect the fish and probably really do believe they are respecting it.

Whenever I talk to a fisherman, they don't really listen to any argument against what they do, but I still go through the motions, because you never know, a tiny seed may get planted. I would rather listen to modern science than old fisherman 'knowledge' that they need to believe in order to enjoy their hobby or carry on with their gruesome livelihood. As the saying goes, it is difficult to change the mind of someone who's income relies on them believing it, but that won't stop me trying.

CHAPTER 94

LOBSTERS DON'T FEEL PAIN

"Life is dear to a mute creature as it is to man. Just as one wants happiness and fears pain, just as one want to live and not die, so do other creatures."

- Dalai Lama

Lobsters and crabs are difficult for us to relate to. They aren't cute like a pig, playful like a rabbit, or as awe inspiring as a great whale. Perhaps this is why we feel there is nothing wrong with tearing them apart or boiling them alive. For years, researchers have said that Lobsters don't feel pain. But is this true? The most recent findings say it's not, so hopefully it will now be easy to change your mind on the age old belief that lobsters and crabs don't feel pain.

I will always remember when I was a young 17 year old in Royal Navy Chef School, not being happy with the way lobsters were cooked. Seeing a real, fully formed and live creature being stabbed in the head and then boiled, just didn't feel right. A rack of lamb, side of beef, even a whole fish, didn't strike these chords though. Having a lifeless form in front of me, already killed and butchered, removed me from the horror of meat and fish production.

Luckily I didn't have to kill my own lobster; even back in 1996, the RN had budgets to maintain. But I saw first hand what was required to get a lobster bisque or Thermadore onto the plate, and I didn't like it one bit. During the 6 years I spent as a Chef, I am pleased to say I never had to kill a lobster or crab myself, but I did serve it and I did cook a lot of meat and poultry. It's difficult looking back when I wasn't a vegetarian or vegan and I'm ashamed of myself for not making the connection much earlier. If I knew then what I know now, would I have chosen a different path? I believe so.

Unfortunately, not all lobsters are stabbed in the head before being cooked. Most are thrown into a boiling pot of water and are literally boiled alive. It can take minutes for them to die in this awful, horrific way. When they hit the boiling water they react by flicking their tail and writhing in the water. You can hear them scraping on the sides of the pot, desperate to be free from an unimaginable fate. Chefs will tell you that they feel no pain, or they go into shock straight away, it's just a reaction. Their reaction seems to be similar to how any sentient being would react. How do they know there is no pain being felt? How do they know these are not sentient beings?

If we want to eat something, then shouldn't we experience or - at the very least - see where it comes from and the process it goes through to get onto our plate and into our stomachs? I was a vegetarian when I first watched the documentary called 'Earthlings'. It showed how animals are treated by humans and how meat, eggs, fish and dairy are produced. It was difficult to look at and comprehend all the terrible things that go on. If everyone watched what is involved in the meat, egg, fish and dairy industries then I am 100% convinced there would be many, many more vegans in this world.

So what does the most recent science say? A study looking at pain in crustaceans found that, "The inhibition by a local anaesthetic is similar to observations on vertebrates and is consistent with the idea that these crustaceans can experience pain."Another study looking at pain experience in hermit crabs found, "The results are consistent with the idea of pain in these animals."

The reality is, that the studies that have been conducted in the past that say lobsters and crabs don't feel pain, have presented conclusions they just can't prove. As stated in a report by Norwegian scientists, titled, 'Sentience and Pain in invertebrates,' "A definite answer to pain in invertebrates may be difficult to find. In the meantime, efforts should be made to maintain these animals in the most appropriate way during handling and confinement, giving them the benefit of doubt in situations that have a potential to cause pain and stress."

The theme is that behaviours of crustaceans in pain experiments, are observed to be consistent with our current understanding of pain. What more do we need to know to tell us they may well feel pain and that boiling them alive is just barbaric and unacceptable? The only way to stop this is to stop eating crabs and lobsters! Choosing a vegan plant based diet is the best way to protest against this awful practice. We don't need to eat these creatures anymore. All our proteins, vitamins, and minerals are available in plant-based foods. Everything we need to be healthy is available now, so why choose unnecessary pain, suffering and torture, just to satisfy our taste buds?

CHAPTER 95

EGGS FROM PETS

"Life is dear to a mute creature as it is to man. Just as one wants happiness and fears pain, just as one want to live and not die, so do other creatures."

- Dalai Lama

Eating eggs is cruel. The ordeal that farmed chickens go through just for us to eat their eggs is terrible. But what about eating eggs from rescued chickens we have as pets?

I never realised what went on and used to be all pleased with myself eating eggs from a local farm where the chickens roamed free and appeared to be having a great life. While I ate the free range cornish eggs, I never thought about all the processed foods I consumed that had dried egg or some kind of egg in them. The reality is that the egg products used in most convenience and processed foods don't come from a nice rural Cornish farm. They come from battery farmed chickens. These battery farmed chickens are featherless, have had their beaks cut off or burned off, and often grow too heavy too quickly so their bones cannot develop in time to hold the weight and their little legs can break under the pressure. Lying broken on the metal grating floor, these poor chickens are trampled on by their neighbours and can't make it to the water or food, so they die a slow painful death whilst lying in their own mess and anguish.

I've never even thought about where the male chickens are? What happens to them is absolutely disgusting. Once sorted, new born hatchlings are separated into males and females and the males are either sent along a conveyer belt to meet their gruesome end in the cogs of a grinding machine or they are 'humanely' gassed. Humanely - what an awful misuse of the word. In my mind, there is no humane way to gas a baby chick to death or grind it up alive into a feathered bloody pulp. It has been documented that chicks have even just been bagged up in thick plastic sacks and left to slowly suffocate.

The whole process is sick. Male chickens lucky enough to make it past the grinder have their sperm 'collected' by humans who then artificially inseminate the females. Some have called this rape, and if you take a moment to mull it over, it's hard to disagree. Only one lucky rooster is required to impregnate a flock of hens. Too many roosters cause damage to the hens and they can be aggressive to each other. The risk for damaging the goods is too high for the farms to take by having too many roosters. As we discuss in previous sections, some poultry are bred to have such large breasts that they cannot even breed naturally if they wanted to.

Imported foods include eggs produced in shocking farms with no animal rights whatsoever. We happily consume them and assume that because we have some standard of animal husbandry in the UK then all foodstuffs sold here will conform. It's just not the case. The thought of eating an egg now makes me feel sick, I am not exaggerating one bit. Is an egg really worth all of this suffering? If it is, then what does that make us as human beings? Are we monsters? Think about it, we grind live baby male chicks to death just because they are male!

But surely if we keep hens as Pets, then we can eat their eggs? If you are going to eat eggs then this is probably the best way to do it, and if you've rescued those chickens from a farm or certain death then even better. However, those eggs are not ours. They belong to the chicken. As a vegan, no animal product is acceptable.

Left alone, the chickens will eat their own eggs, much like rabbits eat their own droppings to extract the nutrients their bodies need. It takes a lot of calcium from them to lay an egg and so they can reclaim it through eating the shell. Once you take away the egg from the chicken she is primed to lay another, so leaving the eggs alone will give the chickens a break.

Through domestication we have selected the best and most frequent 'layers' generation after generation until their laying frequency and behaviour is totally different from their wild cousins. Farms manipulate the lighting, temperature and even withhold food to induce laying. Once the exhausted and malnutritioned chicken stops laying at an 'acceptable' rate, she is killed and her tired old body is sold for boiling up or for animal food. Often, battery farmed rescued hens will still continue to lay even if you leave the eggs alone. But the eggs are still hers and the thought of eating her period is not an appetising one.

Wild birds only lay eggs during a specific breeding season and when sufficient food is available for their young. Once impregnated by a male, the bird will lay eggs until her nest is full. The sperm can remain in the chicken for up to three weeks with all eggs produced in that time being fertilised. So the egg a day is not a natural occurrence but is forced onto the chicken by careful breeding and environmental manipulation. If chickens eggs are left with them, then they will eat them or just let them go to waste, and their laying frequency will decrease over time. The egg industry has had such an impact on us that we believe that if a chicken isn't laying an egg a day then there must be something wrong with her. So if we leave the chickens alone and don't take their eggs then we allow them to reclaim those nutrients and not cause them to lay as frequently.

So after all this there are a few eggs abandoned and the chickens show no interest in them, then what? There is still the issue of health. Eggs are so bad for you that it is against the law in the US to say that eggs are 'nutritious' or 'safe' because they just aren't! Eggs are not nutritious and salmonella from them poisons over a hundred thousand Americans each year. To say they are nutritious or safe would be false advertising.

Eggs are very high in cholesterol with 215 to 275 mg of cholesterol per egg yolk. To put this into perspective, a big mac with fries has 75mg of cholesterol, a third of one simple egg. It is only recommended that if you are healthy you should only have 300mg per day. If you suffer from diabetes, heart disease or have high cholesterol, then you should only have 200mg! One egg will take you over this threshold and actually harm you. Our body creates all the cholesterol we need, so adding more to it on a daily basis can't be good for us.

Not eating eggs doesn't mean you still can't enjoy cake, pancakes, and many other foods. We regularly make Vegan Chocolate Cake, Vegan Banana & Date Cake, Vegan Cupcakes, basically any style of cake. We make Vegan pancakes, vegan scones, vegan pastries, tarts, quiches, and sauces. You don't even need eggs to make scrambled eggs! There are thousands of Vegan alternative recipes to everything we like. The Vegan chocolate cake we make is better than most egg based cakes. It's light and moist, and keeps for a long time. The ingredients are all cheap and convenient and the method is super easy.

The reality is we just don't need eggs to make most of the foods we love and enjoy. We have been fooled for decades. Eating eggs is bad for our health and the chickens health, so I have to wonder:

Why do we eat them at all?
Why are we led to believe they are good for us?
Why aren't eggs thought of as an unhealthy food?
Why would anyone want to eat a period?

CHAPTER 96

WOOL MUST BE OK?

"To use for our exclusive benefit what is not ours is theft."
- Jose Marti

Surely wool is ok? After all, if we don't shear the sheep they will get too hot and maggots can grow in their fleece.

Sheep are present in countries that are not native to them because we put them there. We have selectively bred them to produce more and more wool, just as we have done with cows and their milk production or chickens with their eggs. If we didn't domesticate the sheep and interfere with the natural breeds, these sheep wouldn't be in hot countries where they would need to be sheared in the first place.

Now the argument that sheep are not killed for their wool is valid, but they still suffer. Perhaps not all sheep raised for wool will suffer, but the majority certainly do. We won't know where our wool has come from, or how the sheep were treated. They are sheared roughly and the workers who have to shear them are rough and careless. They have to shear a certain quota within a certain time and to do this the sheep's welfare is not a priority, it just can't be. The sheep are roughly handled, pinned down, and often cut.

When the sheep get old, they are still slaughtered and can end up as cheap mutton or certainly in dog food. The end always seems to be the same for these poor animals, death at the slaughter house followed by consumption by humans or the animals we place above them and keep as our pets.

The sheep do not give us their wool and do not ask to be bred in environments that are not natural for them to be in. We take it from them. The bottom line is, any exploitation is wrong and any cruelty and abuse is unacceptable. When we go vegan, we don't give up anything, we just stop taking that which is not ours to take.

CHAPTER 97

WE NEED ZOOS

"The caged eagle become a metaphor for all forms of isolation, the ultimate in imprisonment. A zoo is prison."

- Nadine Gordimer

Surely zoos are good for animals, without them many species would be extinct. The conservation work the zoos do is crucial; isn't it?

The idea that zoos are educational and are key for conservation is not a convincing one for me. I don't agree with zoos one bit. Do we need to keep lions, apes, and camels in a zoo to protect them? I would argue (though I have no way of proving it) that most people are inspired to work in conservation or animal welfare because of their love for seeing animals in the wild and in their natural habitats, not because they have observed a poor bear pacing around a small enclosure in a Dallas zoo, for example.

Zoos may well portray an educational experience, but they are nothing more than prisons for the animals. True conservation takes place in the field not in tourist attractions and cages in countries that are nothing like the country of origin for the animals. We can educate just as effectively through videos, books, movies, and travel, so we just don't need zoos to act as the main place to educate people about animals.

Looking at a monkey swinging in a tyre, hanging from a single piece of wood and a small info card on the front of his or her cage does nothing to portray the wonder of the animal in their natural habitat. It is so sad to see animals confined in small areas to live out their lives just to entertain us. People will visit a zoo convinced they are animal lovers. They will think they are helping to protect a species of monkey or wild cat and then take a break from their good work to go and eat another animal in the on site Zoo restaurant. As with all animal exploitation, the only animals that benefit are the humans.

CHAPTER 98

HORSE RIDING

"Innocence is thought charming because it offers delightful possibilities for exploitation."

- Mason Cooley

The argument against horse riding is very similar to the argument against eating the eggs from pet hens, and is a much debated topic within vegan circles. Some vegans think it is ok to ride horses and say they share a special bond with their horse. They even say their horse likes to be ridden and that they look forward to it. I have even read comments on social media that people can actually 'talk' to their horse in some psychic way, and their horse let's them know they want to go on a ride. The skeptic in me is not convinced by this I'm afraid.

I take the approach that all animal exploitation is wrong and that includes riding on the back of one. As with eating meat, I have been guilty of riding horses and other animals in the past too, so I am not preaching from my own 'high horse', I am just trying to help others learn from my mistakes.

Is having a horse just like having a dog or cat? I would say that if you rescue the horse then, just like a dog or cat, you are taking it from a bad situation and giving a chance at a peaceful life. Buying a horse from a breeder, however, cannot be acceptable, as you would be funding a business that is entirely built on the exploitation of animals. If you decide to ride a horse, whether from rescue or business transaction, then that's when the rescue or compassionate purchase moves from an act of compassion to one of purchase for exploitation. Instead of riding the horse, just let them run in a field or go for a walk with them. I'm sure you don't have to ride horses to connect with them and to ride them is to give yourself a good time, not the horse.

CHAPTER 99

VEGANS HAVE PETS

"The world is a dangerous place, not because of those who do evil, but because of those who look on and do nothing."

- Albert Einstein

Most vegans will have rescue animals as pets. Abandoned and abused animals are in shelters all around the world, all in need of a kind and loving home. The fact that breeders are producing more animals when so many need homes just doesn't make any sense. They are making a profit from over breeding and animals in breeding farms suffer ill treatment just as farmed animals do.

The pet industry and breeders are adding more and more dogs to locations where there are already huge problems. It's obviously not always their intention and perhaps some breeders breed dogs because they have a passion for a particular breed, but most are only in the breeding business for money. In fact, if breeders were only doing it out of love, then why not give the puppies away, or better still, let them stay with their Mum? If we want to solve the stray and abandoned dog problem, surely the best option has to be to re-home those dogs that have been abandoned before we look to breed more? I think that this is what most Vegans will do. They will seek out an animal that has been abandoned and then give it a loving peaceful life.

I often wrestle with the idea that owning a cat, dog, or any pet is wrong. Is putting a collar and lead on a dog bad? I think it is, but without it, I would put our Alfie dog at risk of being knocked over by traffic when we go out. He never wears a collar when we are at home, and as soon as possible on our country walks, he comes of the lead to run where he wants to. Buying a dog from a breeder is not good when there are so many other dogs already born and abandoned that need a forever home. Alfie was purchased from a breeder, so I am completely guilty of once paying into a system I now so despise. I was ignorant and uneducated, but now I know it's wrong, I can try to do my best to share my mistakes with other people. Our Epic Animal Quest, is all about helping abandoned animals and finding them forever homes with people who might otherwise have gone to a breeder. Now I know better, I am doing everything I can to do better, and I hope by helping others to see how I got it wrong, they will do better too.

A FINAL NOTE

Thank you for purchasing this book and I hope it helps you during your Vegan journey. I would love to hear from you and receive any feedback you have, so please get in touch anytime using the contacts in the next section, About Epic Animal Quest.

Making the choice to be vegan for the animals, our health, our future, and the planet, is one of the most important decisions we can ever make. One we make it, the world is never the same again and we look at things completely differently.

Now that we know better, I believe we all have a responsibility to do better and I hope my book can help with that. I started this book with one short sentence that I truly believe in and that's the one I want to leave you with.

You have the power to change the world.

Thank you

Lee

ABOUT EPIC ANIMAL QUEST

OUR MISSION

Our mission is to lead by example to influence others to show compassion, respect and care for all animals.

Our Main Goals

We want to leave the world better than we found it.
We want to stop contributing to the destruction of the planet.
We want to teach compassion, kindness and care for all living creatures.
We want to promote a Healthy lifestyle.
We want to do everything we can to give our children and future generations a brighter future.

Why Are These Goals Important To Us?

We have children and like all parents we want to give them the best we can. We believe this is not achieved through gifts or money, but rather through real world education, teaching them all about a healthy lifestyle, leading by example, sharing experiences, and spending as much time together as possible.

If we can teach the next generation about compassion and how to show it to all animals, we believe this will have a direct effect on how they treat other people. It will positively effect the environment and their own health and well being. By showing compassion for animals we will automatically instil compassion for our fellow humans and bring everyone together regardless of race, colour, nationality or ethnicity.

Compassion for all animals brings with it benefits to diet and health, the environment, and our relationships with other people.

Animals and The Environment

We have lost our connection with most animals and have commodified many of them. Animals are treated as mere objects and are considered as a just a product to be traded and profited from. This has to stop and we have to reconnect with all animals and stop all cruelty wherever we find it.

Starting with our own children and the next generation, we believe we can set them up to start putting right the terrible things we have done to other animals and our planet. There is too much at stake to just carry on regardless. The oceans could be empty of fish by 2050, the rainforests are being destroyed at a sickening pace (2 football fields every second), and over 3000 animals are killed every second just for us to eat them.

The World Is Full Of Good People

We want to highlight the great work that good people are doing everyday and the sacrifices they make with no benefit to themselves. The world can be a cruel and heartless place, but there are millions of good, kind, generous people out there that we want to meet and share their stories with you and the world.

Remove The Wool From Our Eyes

We live in a polarised world. We see cruelty and hate at one end and compassion and love at the other. In between lies the middle ground where most of us carry on with our normal lives without really thinking about the bigger picture. There is nothing wrong with this, it is, after all, how we have been brought up and we are continually bombarded with propaganda from the government and the organisations that own and control our media, our food, and our pharmaceuticals. We believe what we have been told by our parents and authorities and do what we believe is right for us and our family based on what we've been told.

We all have the ability to reason, debate, question, investigate, and explore yet we can so easily be manipulated to follow the crowd, do as we are told, and be convinced by others who try to make us follow their agenda.

We have realised that the world is nothing like the one we were told about. Our human race acts as if it is far more advanced than any other species. We are technologically incomparable but how do we behave ethically? We treat other species as if they are nothing, worthless, and ours to neglect, eat, abuse, and show a complete disregard for. We may be technologically superior but we are lacking ethically, morally, and compassionately.

The internet has developed so much now, so much that we can now remove the wool that has been so cleverly pulled over our eyes. We can see clearly for the first time. We can see how we've have been misled, mis guided, and out right lied to for so long but now it's time we take back our planet, save our fellow animals, and move forward as a cohesive planet of ethical and compassionate human beings.

Life Is For Living

Life doesn't have to be a set pattern of school, college, university, job, retirement, die. You don't have to work for 40-50 years looking forward to retirement only to find that you either don't live long enough to retire or you are too ill to enjoy when you get there! The world has changed, for the worst but also for the better. The internet has provided opportunities to bring people together across the continents and we can use this amazing tool to achieve our goals and live a purposeful and exciting life, helping others less fortunate than ourselves (that's all animals including us humans) and promoting compassion. This might well be the only life we get so we don't want to waste it following the norms society guides us towards. We want to leave our mark on the world and make that mark a positive one.

We believe in this so much that we sold our business, sold almost everything we owned, and committed to a life of travel and adventure in our Quest to help as many animals as we can. If we want to stop the destruction of the environment and stop the cruelty to animals, we have to dedicate our lives to this project.

If You Share Our Philosophy Then Join Our Epic Animal Quest.

We want others to follow our quest and join us on our mission to show compassion, respect and care for all animals.

Help us to help the helpless and shine a light on the good people that represent what it really means to be human.

Find us at: www.epicanimalquest.com

Email us: lee@epicanimalquest.com or epicanimalquest@gmail.com

Twitter: http://www.twitter.com/epicanimalquest

Instagram: http://www.instagram.com/epicanimalquest

Pinterest: https://uk.pinterest.com/epicanimalquest/

Facebook: https://www.facebook.com/epicanimalquest/

FURTHER READING

BOOKS

The China Study: The Most Comprehensive Study of Nutrition Ever Conducted and the Startling Implications for Diet, Weight Loss and Long-Term Health by C. Campbell & T. Campbell http://amzn.to/2kVbPqw

How Not To Die by Michael Greger http://amzn.to/2mb3G1i

The Food Revolution: How your diet can help save your life and our world by John Robbins http://amzn.to/2lWViX4

Forks Over Knives by Gene Stone http://amzn.to/2kAQbff

Whole: Rethinking the Science of Nutrition by T. Colin Campbell http://amzn.to/2maU72n

Armageddon: The true cost of cheap meat by Philip Lymbery http://amzn.to/2kASlew

Salt Sugar Fat: How the Food Giants Hooked Us by Michael Moss http://amzn.to/2lWOUPC

Animal Liberation by Peter Singer http://amzn.to/2lxQHKB

The Life You Can Save by Peter Singer http://amzn.to/2mb7mQN

The Mystic Cookfire by Veronika Sophia Robinson http://amzn.to/2kAPLFu

Eat Like You Care by Gary Francione and Anna Charlton http://amzn.to/2lWSauE

Vegan Freak by Bob Torres and Jenna Torres http://amzn.to/2kAR6MF

Why We Love Dogs, Eat Pigs, and Wear Cows by Melanie Jpy Ph.D. http://amzn.to/2maZcrL

Eating Animal by Jonathan Safran Foer http://amzn.to/2kVkpFE

Animal Rights: The Abolitionist Approach by Gary Francione and Anna Charlton http://amzn.to/2lxB1XS

The Quest for a Moral Compass: A Global History of Ethics by Kenan Malik http://amzn.to/2kARoTy

Love, Poverty and War: Journeys and Essays by Christopher Hitchens http://amzn.to/2kVhFZ1

Animal Ethics: The Basics by Tony Milligan http://amzn.to/2kVr2bh

When Elephants Weep by Jeffrey Masson and Susan McCarthy http://amzn.to/2kAUmr6

Dominion: The Power of Man, the Suffering of Animals, and the Call to Mercy by Matthew Scully http://amzn.to/2kVdE73

Why Animals Matter by Marc Bekoff http://amzn.to/2mb9PL1

Rewinding Our Hearts by Marc Bekoff http://amzn.to/2maYoTE

DOCUMENTARIES

We watched pretty much all of Gary Yourofskys videos on youtube and were inspired to take our lives in a completely different direction than anything we had ever dreamed of.

Check out everything by James Aspey on YouTube.

Here are five documentaries we watched that changed how we thought about animals and our relationship with them:

- Earthlings
- Cowspiracy
- Forks Over Knives
- Vegucation

■   Fat, Sick and Nearly Dead

SOME LINKS ABOUT EGGS

This video goes into detail about eggs and health https://www.youtube.com/watch?v=RtGf2FuzKo4

Here is link with further reading and resources which I highly recommend http://nutritionfacts.org/video/who-says-eggs-arent-healthy-or-safe/

Cholesterol study http://www.sciencedirect.com/science/article/pii/S0828282X10704566

SOME LINKS ABOUT MEAT AND CANCER

http://www.animalvisuals.org/data/1mc/

http://www.ewg.org/meateatersguide/at-a-glance-brochure/

http://www.cancercouncil.com.au/21639/cancer-information/cancer-risk-and-prevention/healthy-weight-diet-and-exercise/meat-and-cancer/

http://www.pnas.org/content/112/2/542.abstract

OTHER LINKS OF INTEREST

Italian celebrity chef calls vegans 'members of a sect' and even state he would kill them all! (He really said that, check out the article here).

Adopting a vegan diet will not cause you to suffer from depression according to this study,

Moods are actually affected by diet, and the vegan diet has been suggested to improve your mood in general. This study looked at a specific question about the future, not a general day to day mood, an NCBI study

Surely dairy farmers are not allowed to let any kind of puss enter the milk? Milk Hygiene Guide For Milk Producers by the Food Standards Agency in the UK

To learn more and to research the science of fish and pain: http://www.fishpain.com

This video is a first hand account of what happens to crabs and lobsters in factories in America and elsewhere. VIDEO https://youtu.be/4jgfyd6M-I0

Gary Yourofsky, a prominent animal rights activist and speaker, said, 'If something is not good enough for your eyes, then why is it good enough for your stomach?' http://www.adaptt.org

WEBSITES

Www.epicanimalquest.com

Www.peta.com

Www.adaptt.org

Www.earthlings.com

Www.blackfish.com

Www.vegansociety.com

Www.veganfoodquest.com

Www.mercyforanimals.org

Www.forksoverknives.com

Www.vegucation.com

Www.cowspiracy.com

Www.nutritionfacts.org

Www.cronometer.com

Printed in Great Britain
by Amazon